I would like to thank all of the people that have made this book possible.

Firstly, my husband Steve, who never, ever complains about how much time and money I spend on my many hobbies, or that he has to cook tea because I'm painting, and for the encouragement he gives me.

I want to thank all my other family members who unfailingly support me and tell me 'you can'.

To the members of the Washington Arts Centre watercolour class and oil painting class, I would like to say thankyou for making class time and zoom time so enjoyable.

And last but not least, thankyou to my teacher Vince Cooper, Artist, who has with endless patience, taught me everything I know.

Index

Preface

Still life

Pen and Wash

Painting the dark

The Landscape

Buildings and Landmarks

Wildlife

People

Abstract Art

Thankyou

About the Author

Preface

Firstly, let me make it clear, I am in no way an expert in painting and this book is not intended to teach painting, it is intended as a lighthearted look at my own journey in learning and a little peek at some of the work that I have done.

I have loved arts and crafts since being a very small child colouring princess dresses and drawing pictures of our dog.

Since then I have been involved in many crafts including paper crafts, cross stitch, dress making, quilting, glass and ceramic painting, jewellery making, the list goes on and on as my long suffering husband will tell you.

Thinking of myself as a creative 'jack of all trades, master of none' I didn't have the confidence to tackle what I thought of as 'proper art' like painting, until one day in my mid fifties I decided I had nothing to lose by giving watercolour painting a go.

That's when I joined the class at the Arts Centre Washington with the idea that if I was 'rubbish' at it I didn't have to keep going.

The teacher and other students were so welcoming and friendly that after that first class I never looked back and later also joined the oil painting group.

I haven't set this book out in any sort of linear fashion, the paintings are not in date order, I just wanted to give a flavour of the sort of thing I do. I still tell my teacher 'I can't do it' or 'I don't get it' but I have a go and usually it turns out okay, and if it doesn't, it's just paper, canvas and paint, no-one's getting hurt by it.

It is my greatest wish that by reading this book, those that think they can't paint or are intimidated by the thought of it, will be inspired to give it a go. Why not, what have you got to lose.

Still Life

Still life is where I started painting, first with watercolour then oil. I did a lot of it and still love it

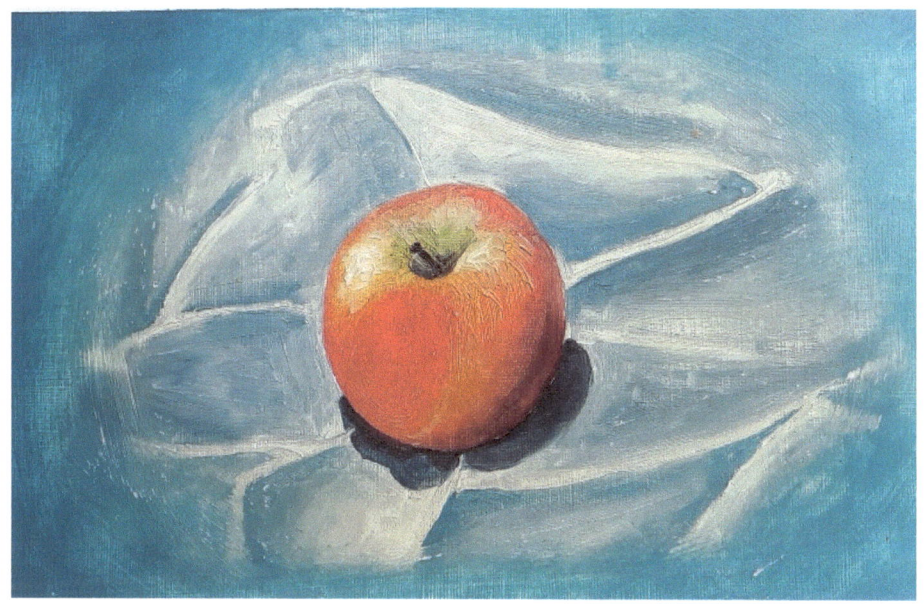

Single red apple **Oil on oil paper**

My first ever oil painting. I had been watercolour painting for a while but had never tried oils. I decided to start small and after watching a YouTube video I had a go at this. It was quite successful and I was bitten by the bug to do more so I joined the oil painting class at my local Arts Centre in Washington where I had been attending watercolour classes.

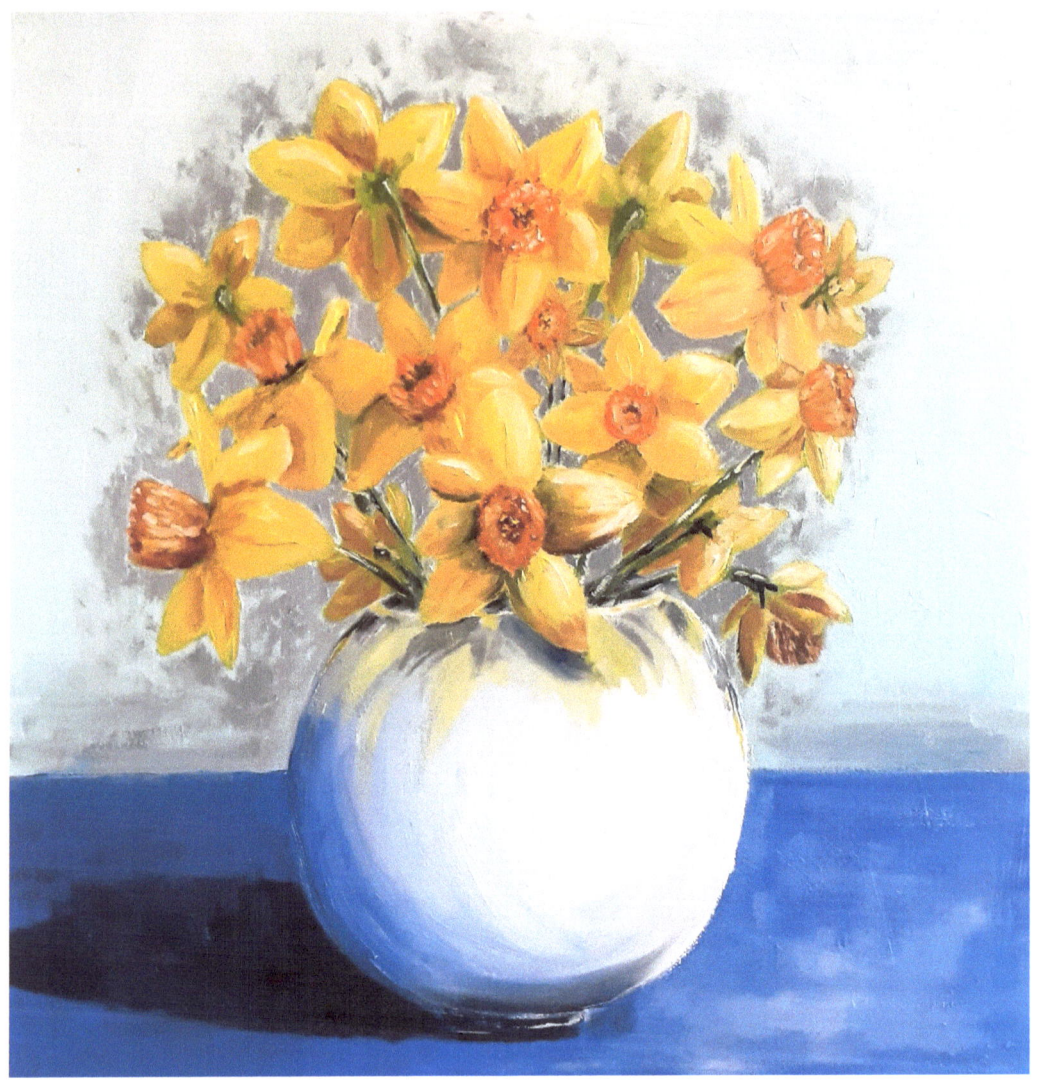

Happy Daffs Oil on canvas, 12" x 12"

I couldn't resist painting this vase of daffodils, it would be criminal not to. Daffodils make me happy.

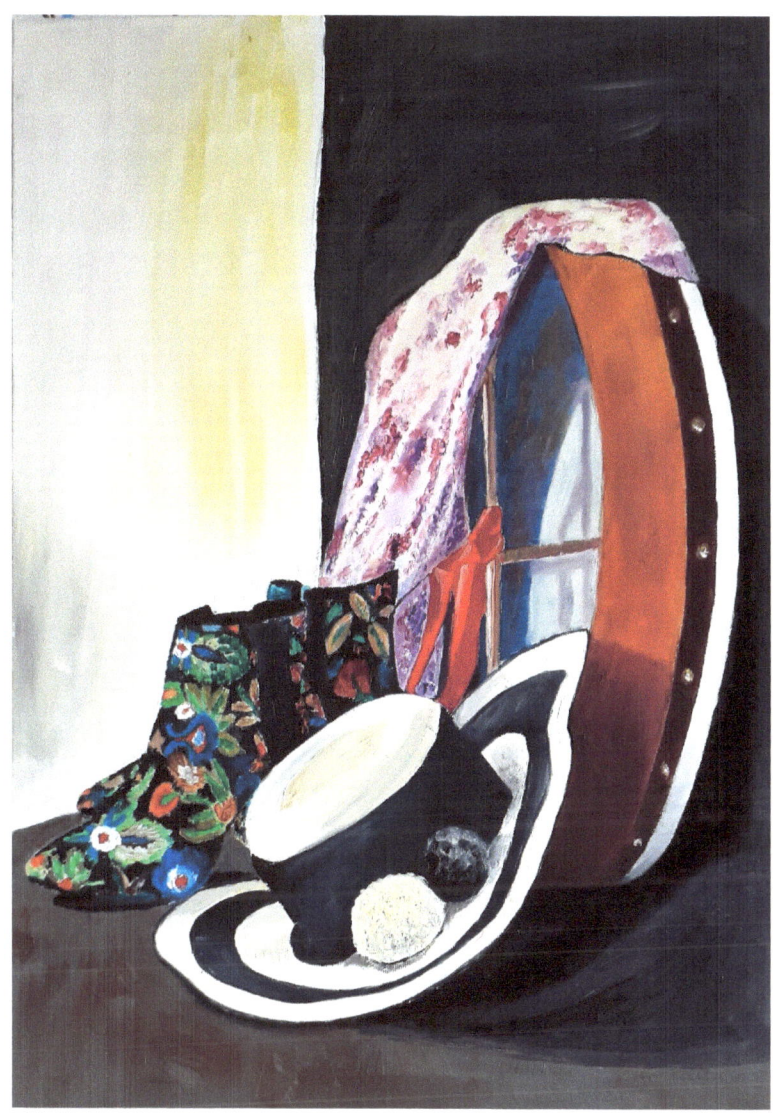

Hat and drum **Oil on Canvas, A2**

Hat and Drum was the first painting I had to tackle when I started at the oil painting class. It was very daunting at first but I got lots of help and encouragement from both Vince and the rest of the class.

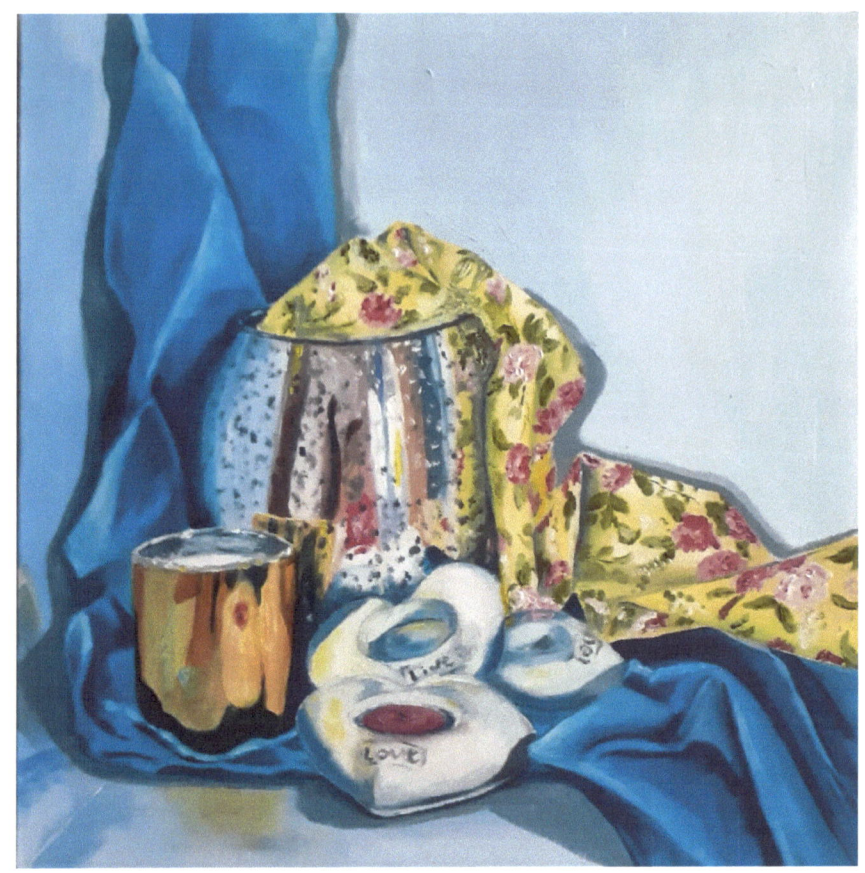

Blue and yellow still life **Oil on canvas, 12" x 12"**

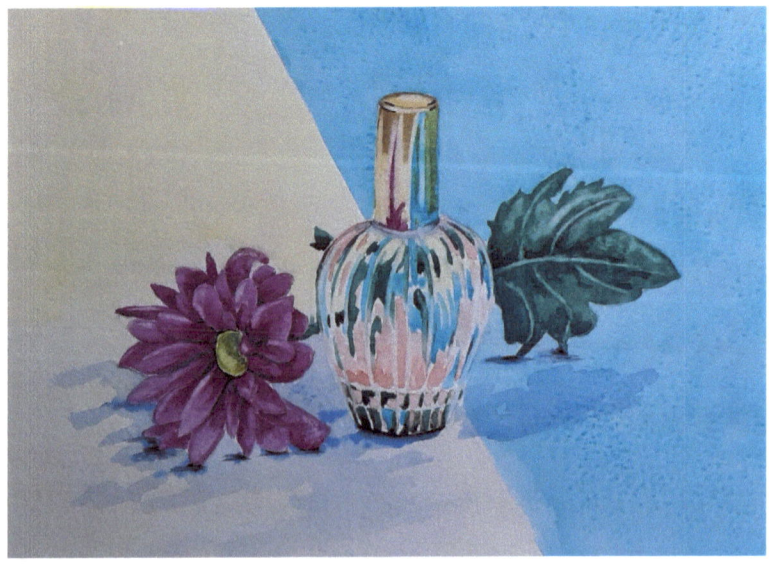

Perfume bottle and flower **Watercolour on paper**

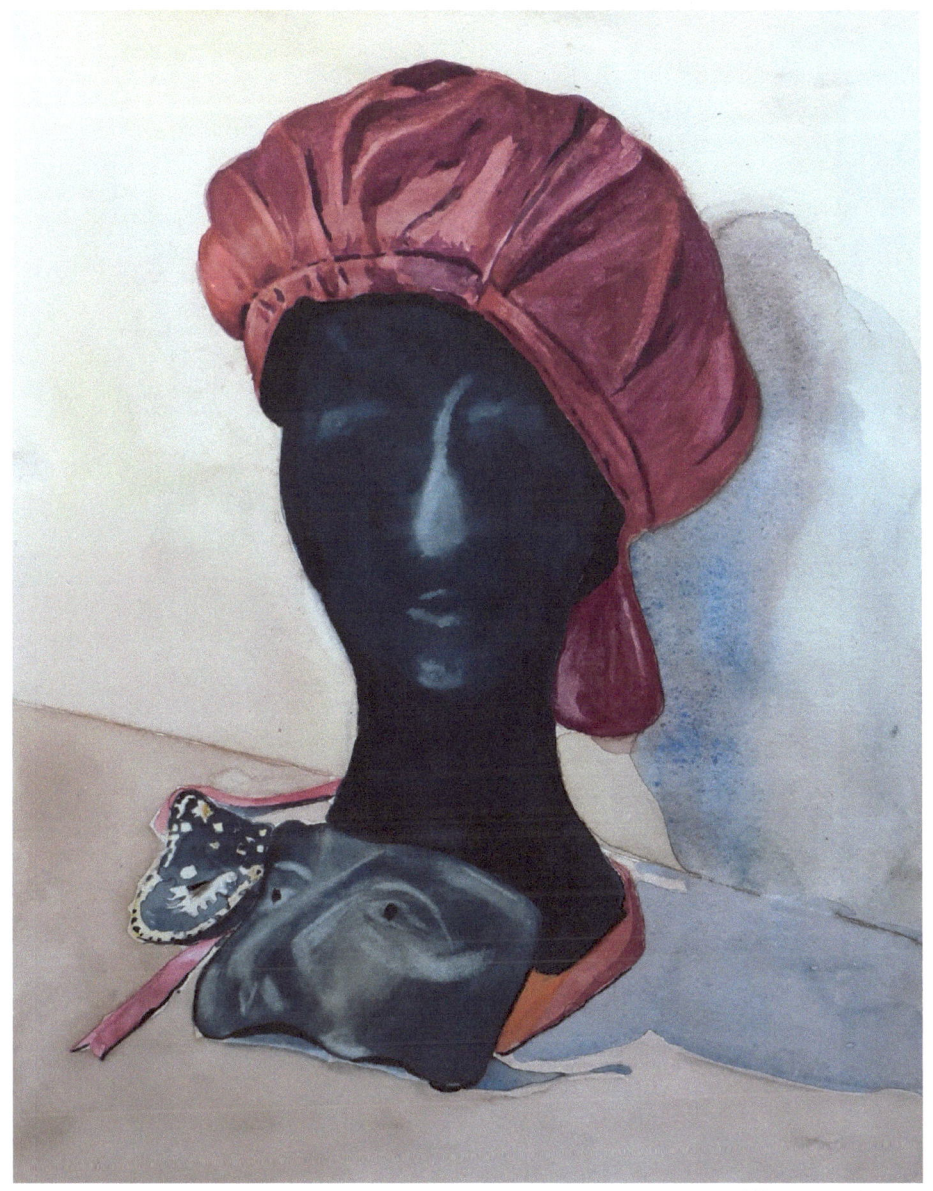

To get ahead — Watercolour

This was a challenging class setup, getting the paint dark enough for the model head and making the hat look soft was difficult, but it was well worth the effort.

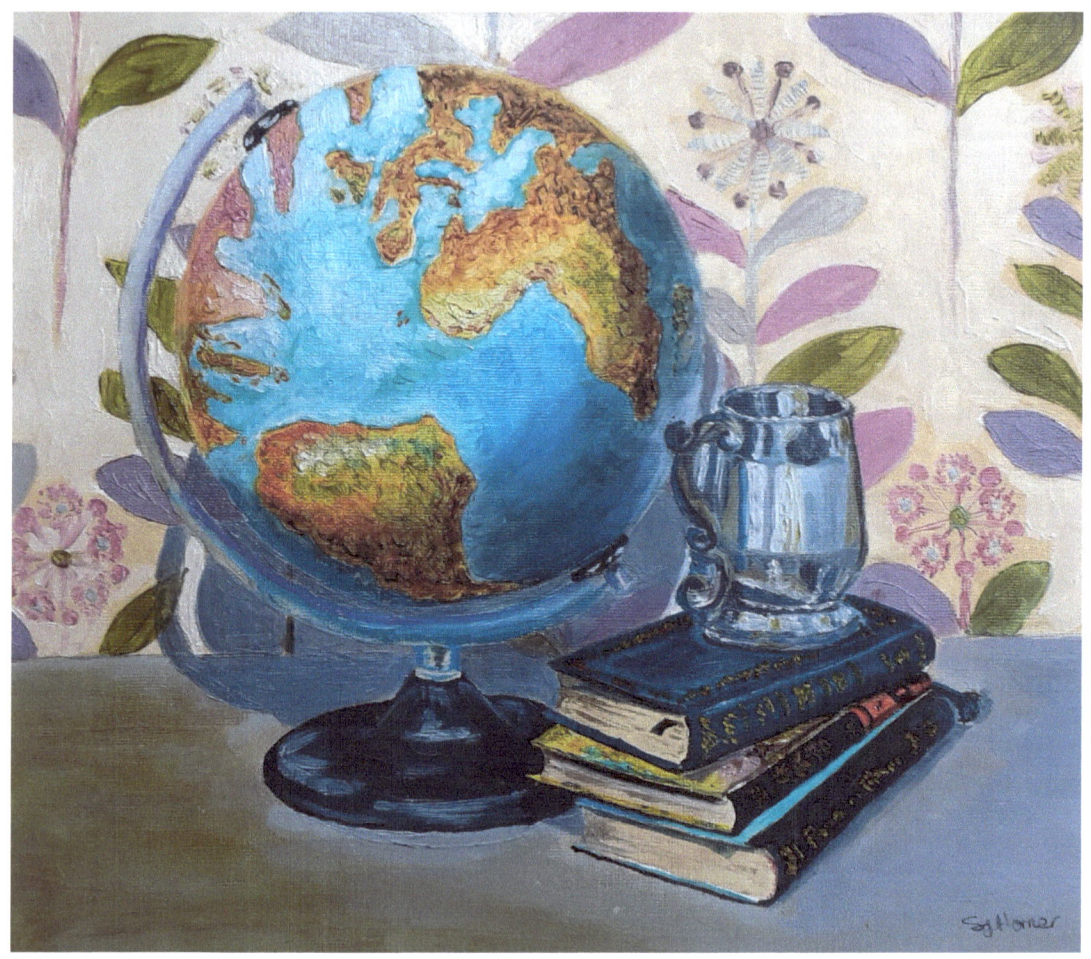

The globe   Oil on oil paper

A collection of items from around the house that I pulled together and set up on the kitchen table to create a still life that kept me busy one rainy weekend.

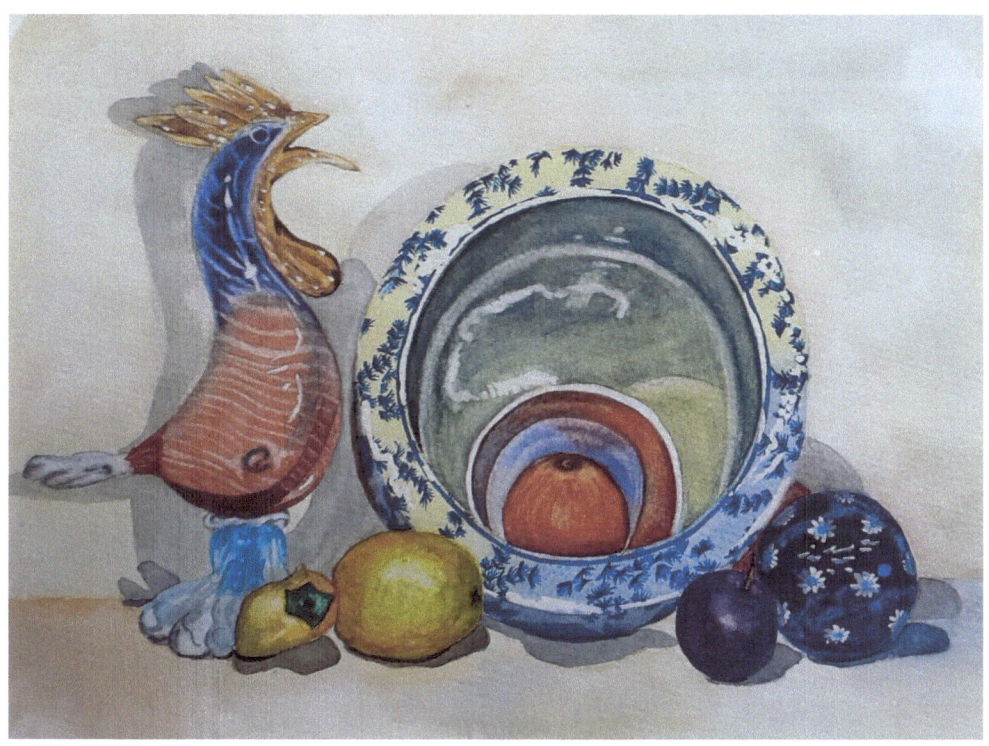

The glass cockerel — Watercolour

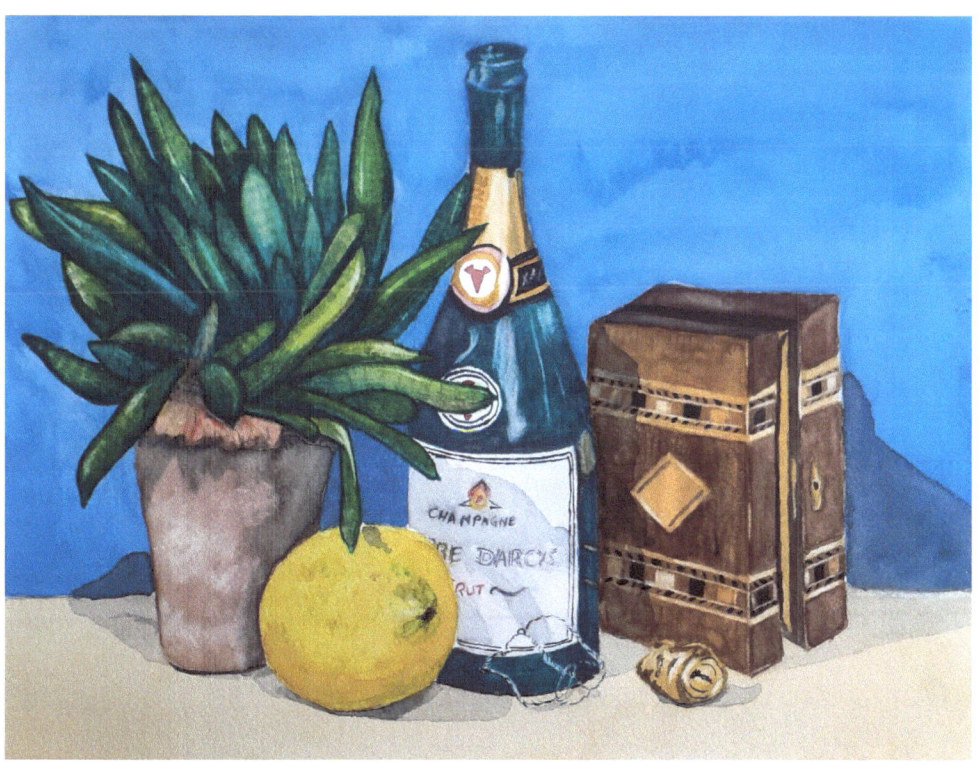

The gentlemen's club — Watercolour

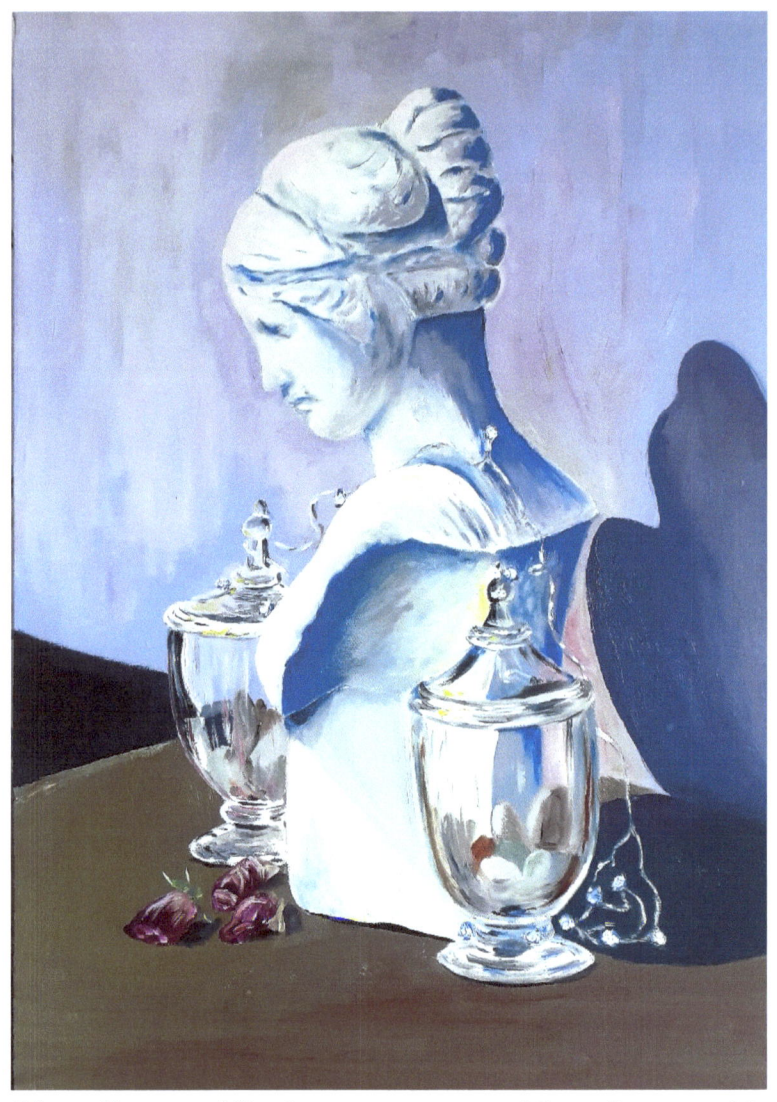

Glass Urns and Bust   **Oil on Canvas, A2**

Another classroom project. It's a challenge to portray glass with paint but I think this works. Also the plaster bust has lots of colour reflected on it but must still be read as white.

Never say "I cant find anything to paint" there's always something lying around you can use.

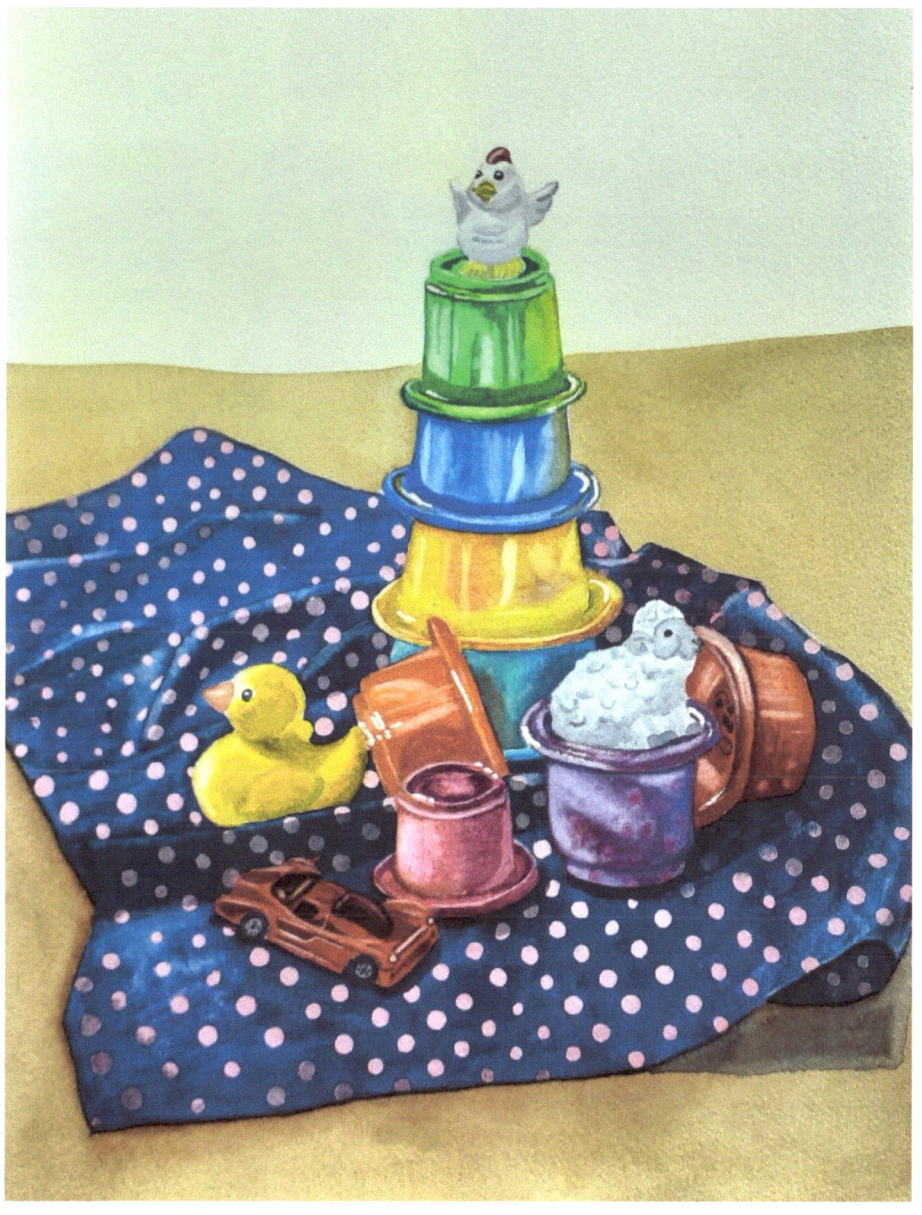

The grandkids are coming   Watercolour

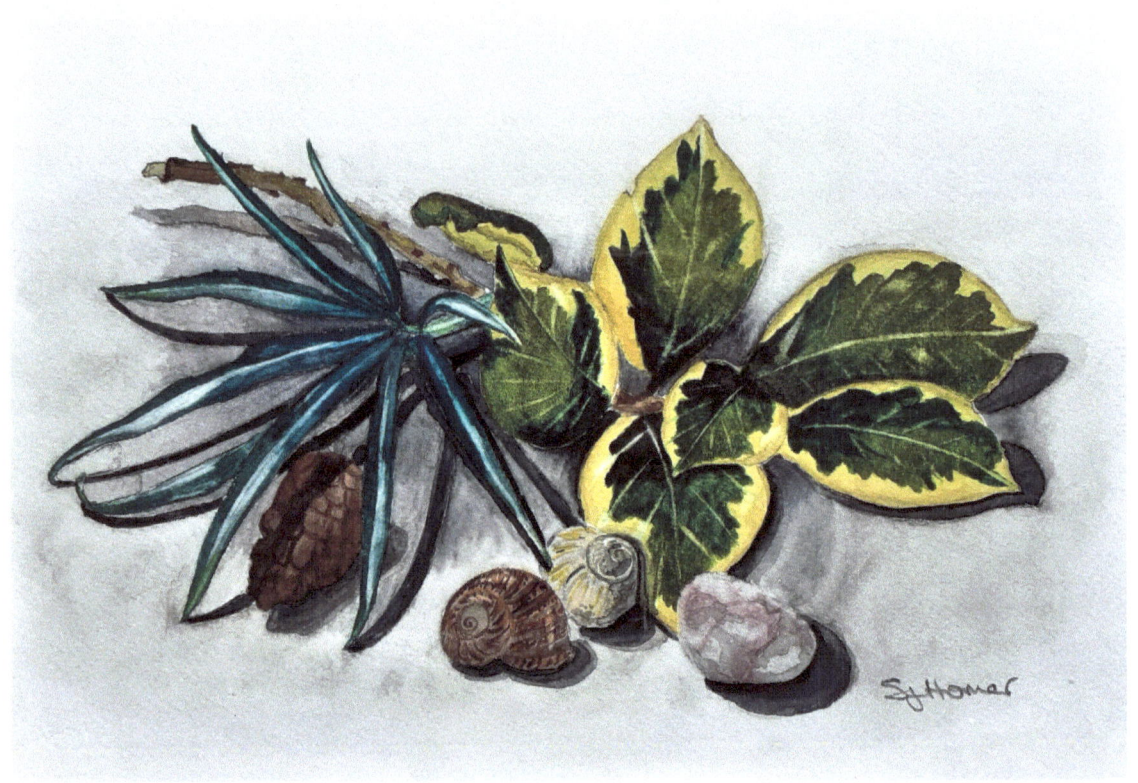

From the Garden **Watercolour**

A scout around the garden provided me with a nice collection to paint this watercolour.

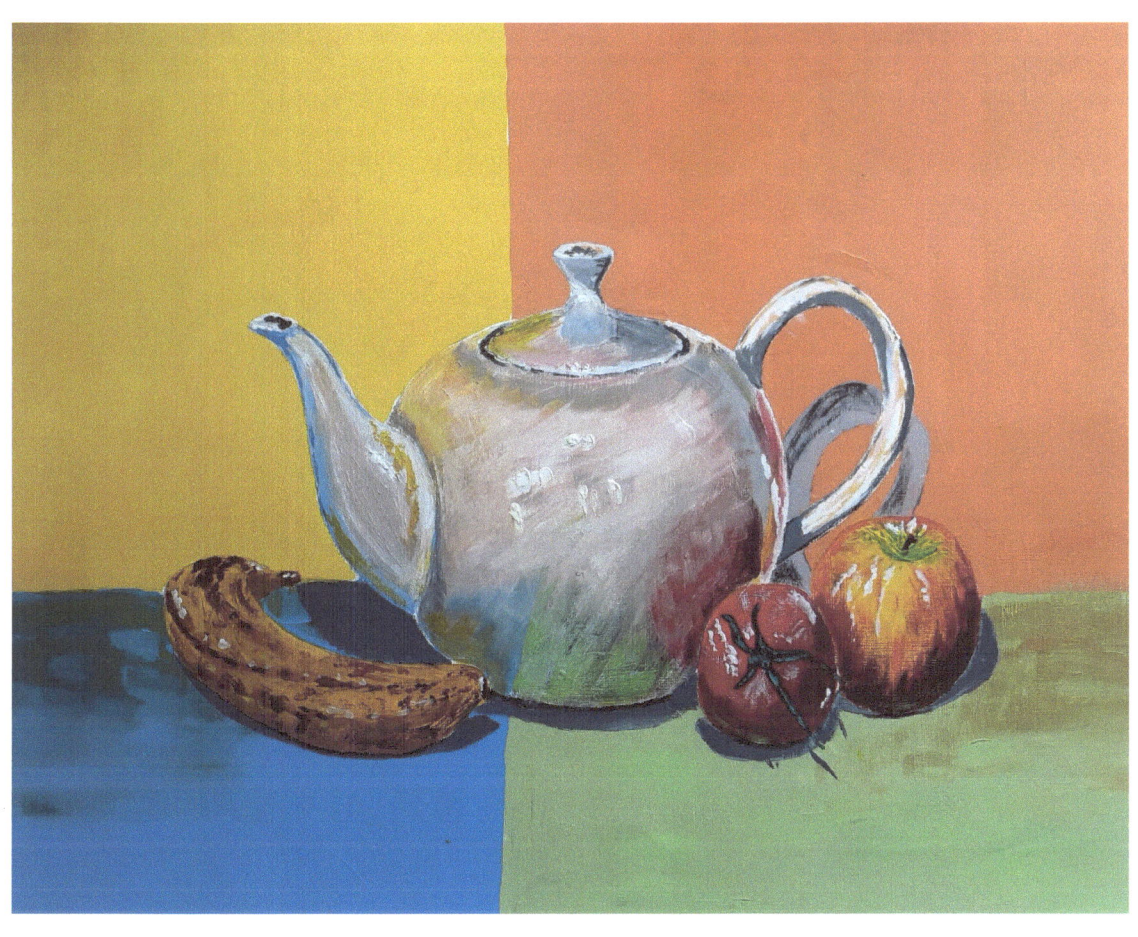

Acrylics on paper, 12" x 16"

Another kitchen table setup, this time using acrylic paint on paper specially designed for the job. I used items readily available in the kitchen and some coloured A4 card for the background and base which I think gives It a retro feel.

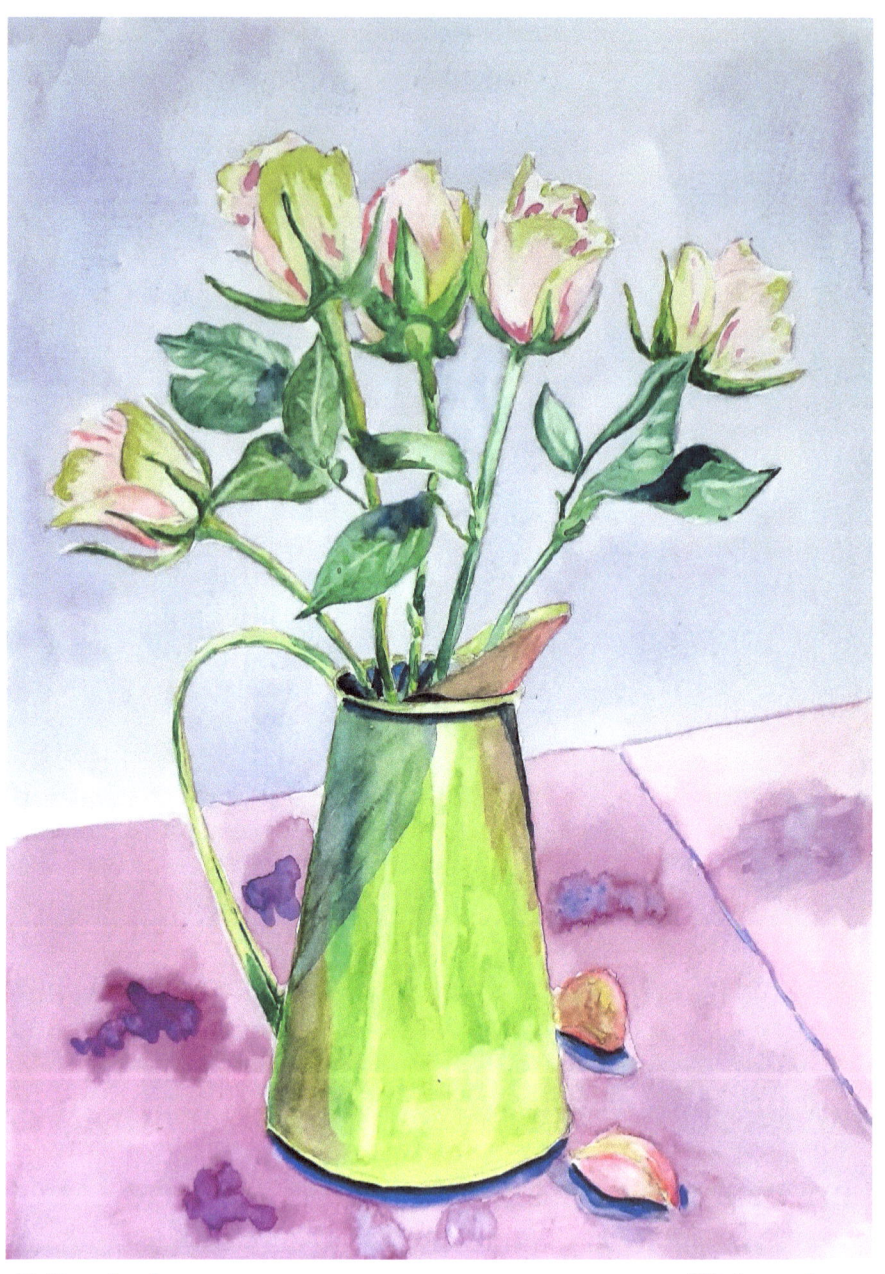

Tulips in Jug   **Watercolour**

A quick and cheerful watercolour that I did in one very relaxing afternoon class.

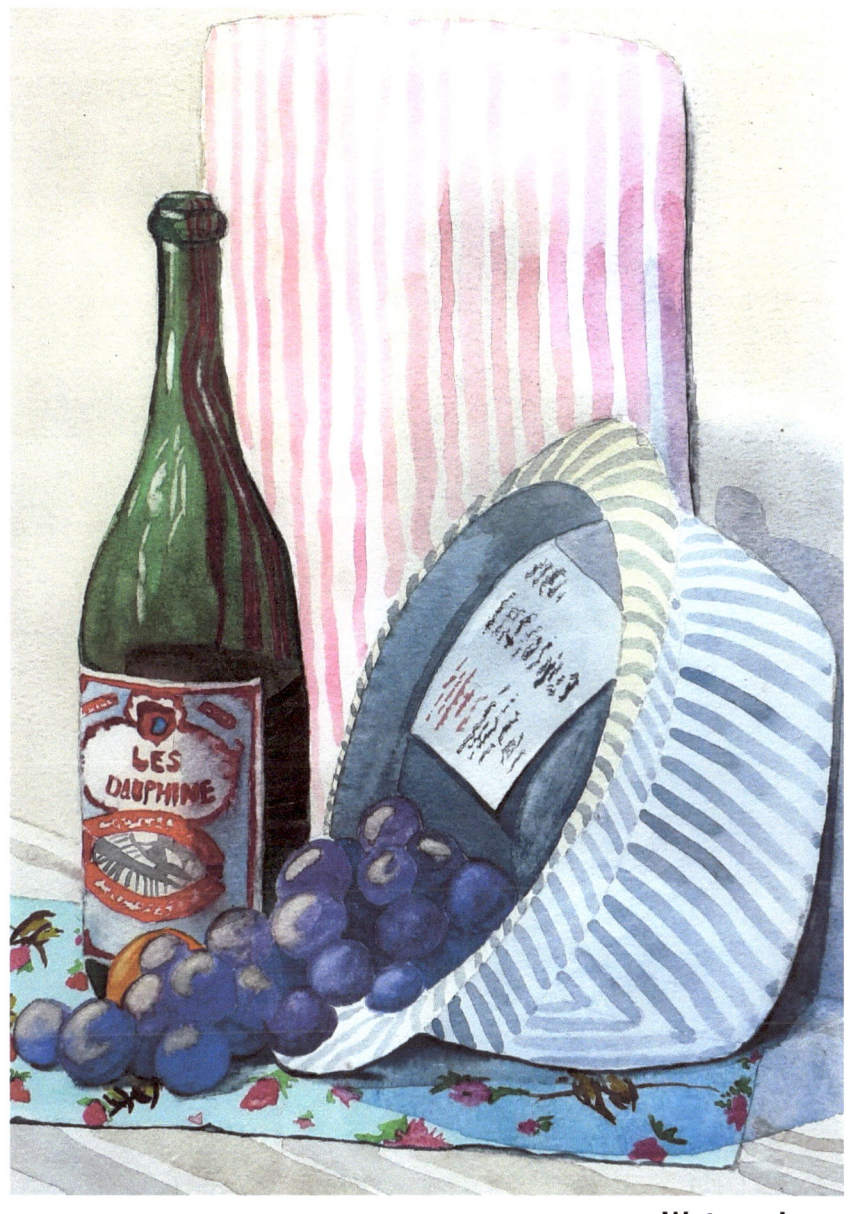

A Class Still life   **Watercolour**

It took several weeks of class time to produce this watercolour, but I was pleased with the final results

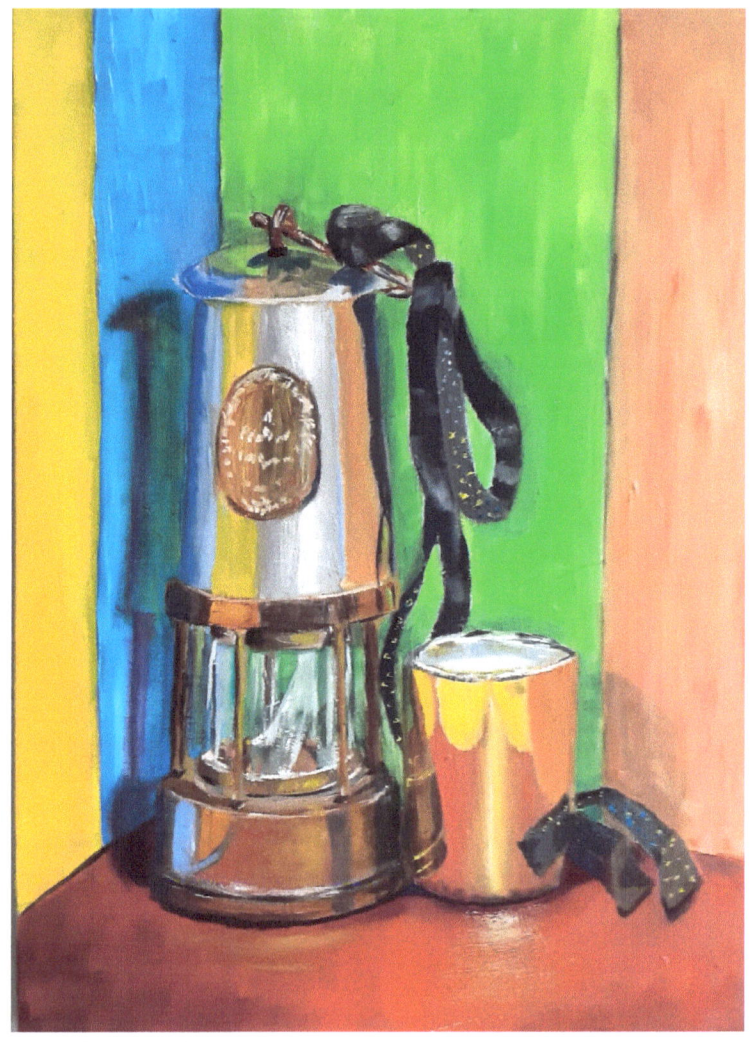

The Miners Lamp Oil on Canvas, 12" x 16"

A random collection of items put together for the sole purpose of having something to paint. I again made use of some A4 coloured card for the base and background.

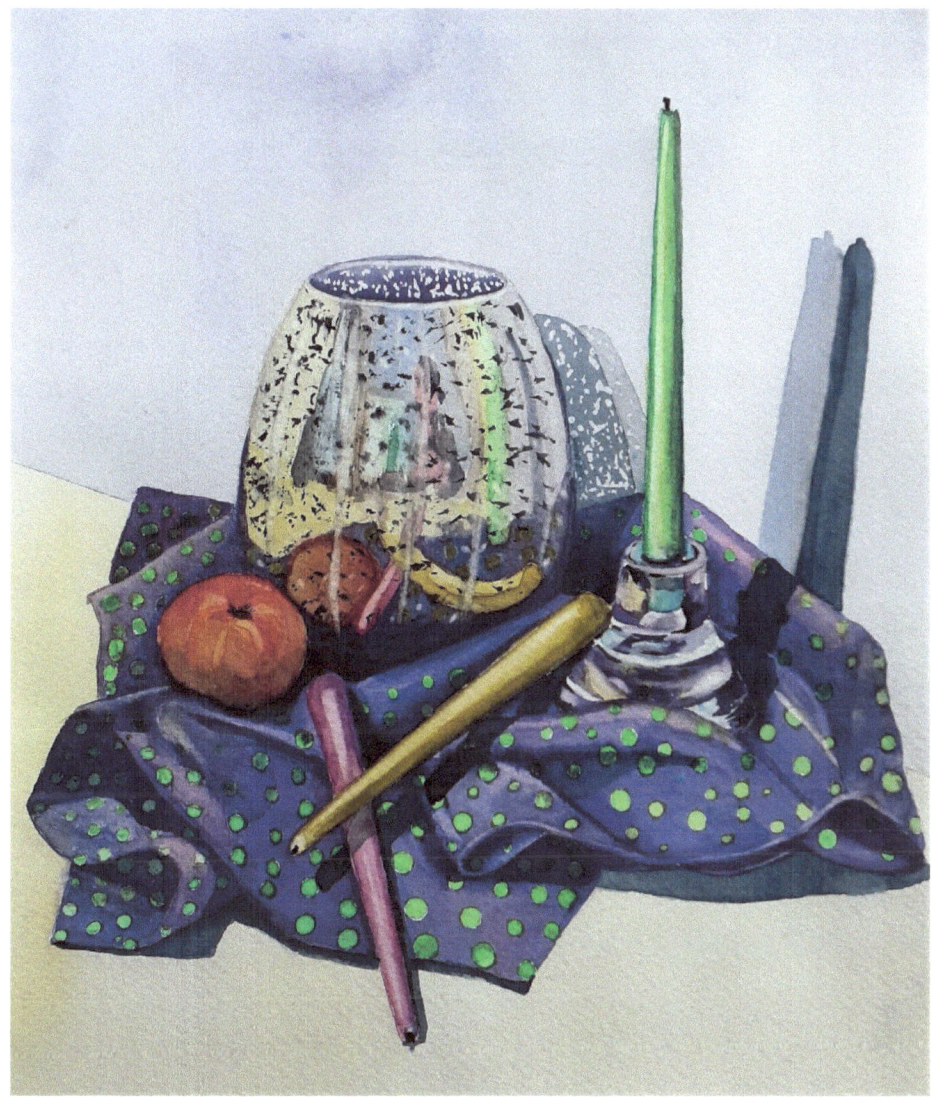

Mirror vase and candles   **Watercolour**

I wanted to practice painting glass and other shiny objects, this setup was perfect for the job, it had the added bonus of the tricky to paint fabric.

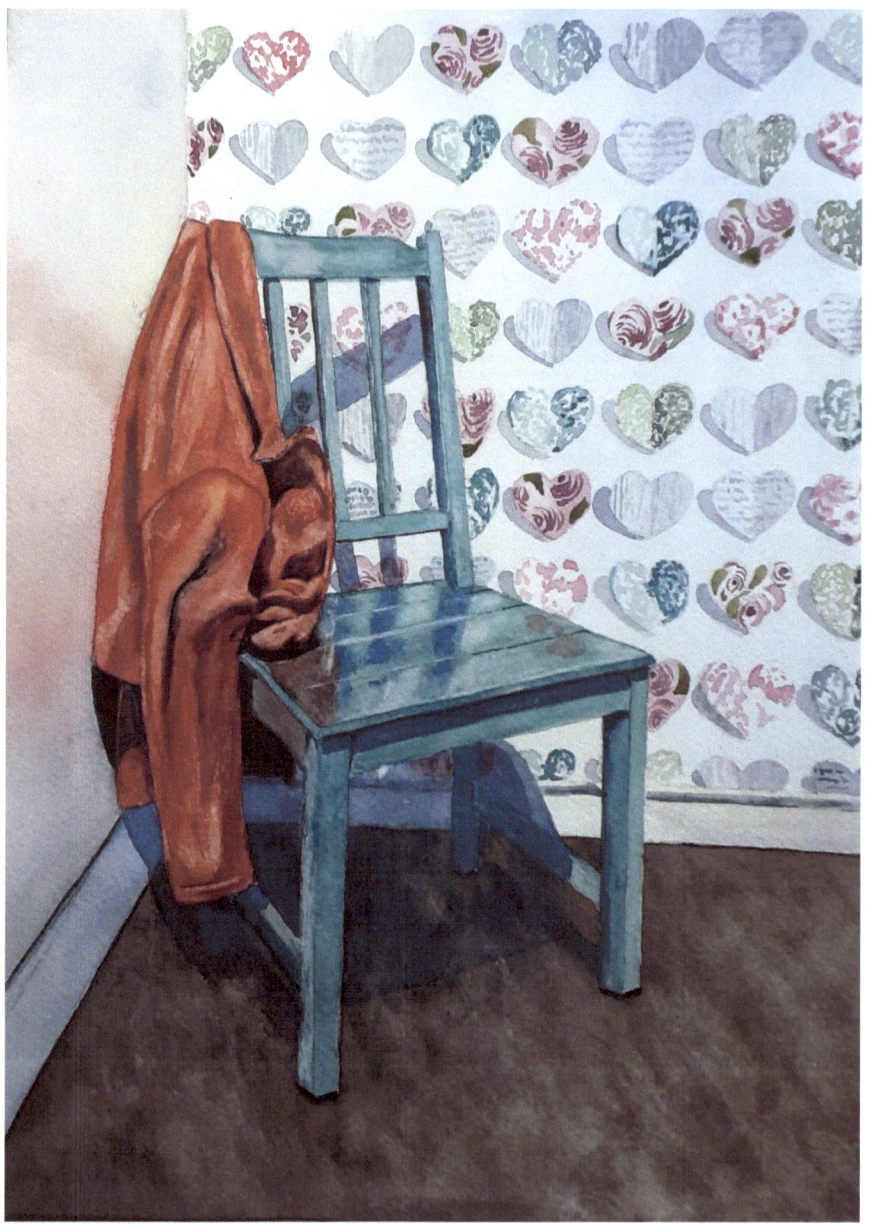

Kitchen Chair   **Watercolour**

Even something as mundane as my kitchen chair can make an impressive painting.

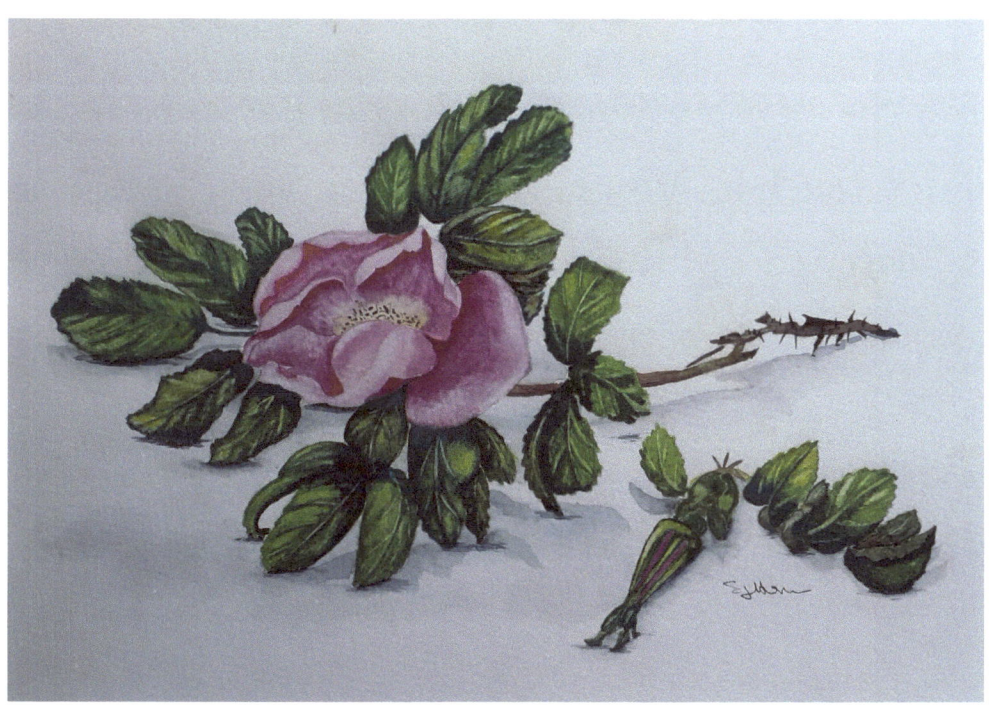

Wild Rose   Watercolour

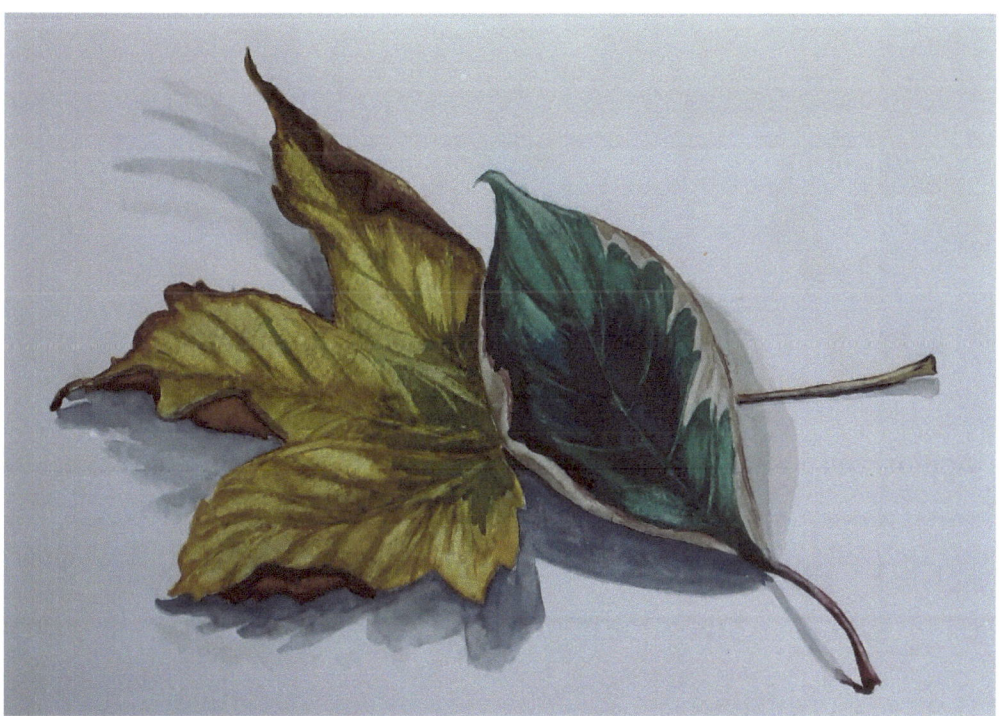

Fallen Leaves   Watercolour

Pen and Wash

Using the pen and wash technique, as encouraged by my art teacher, Vince, has proved very useful and has 'loosened up' my watercolour considerably. It is also quite an effective way of catching detail out in the field.

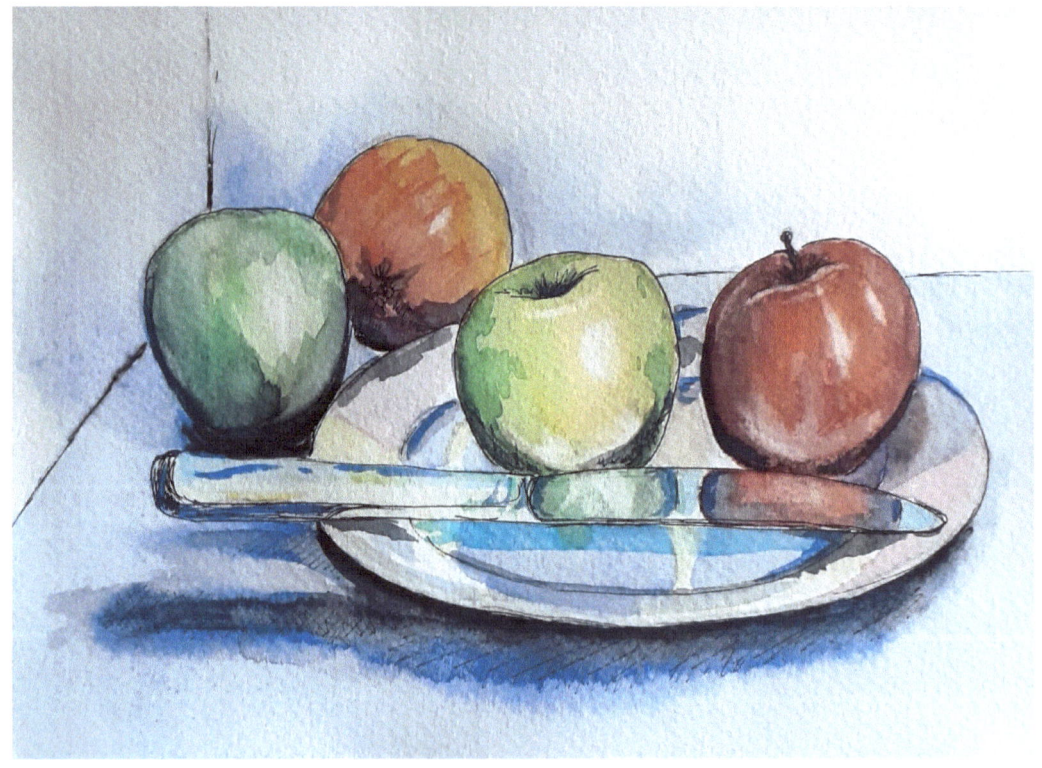

Apples and Plate **Pen and Wash, 2021**

This apples and plate watercolour was captured very quickly using pen and wash. Giving it a bright and fresh feeling.

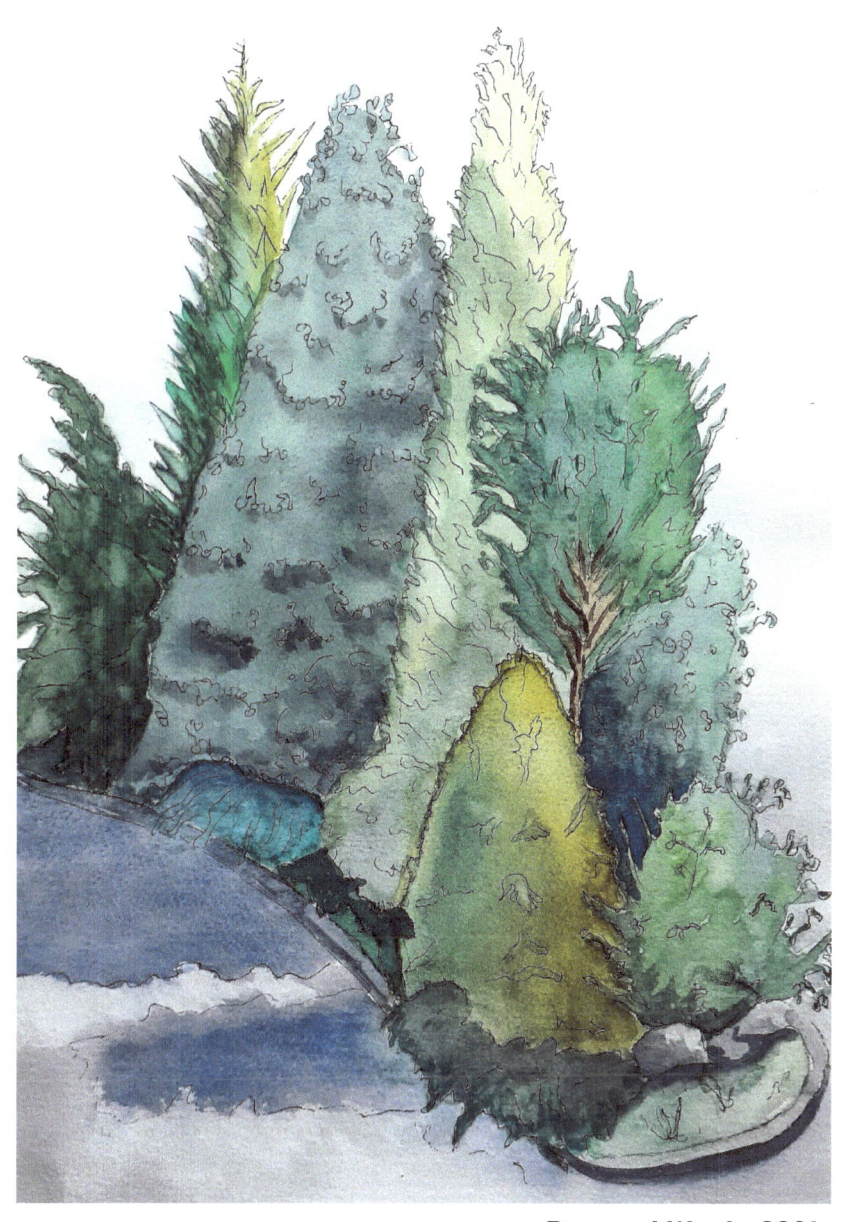

Pen and Wash, 2021

A collection of trees on a small traffic island on a housing estate. This was actually my first attempt at pen and wash.

Here's those daffodils again, I can't resist them. This time I use pen and wash.

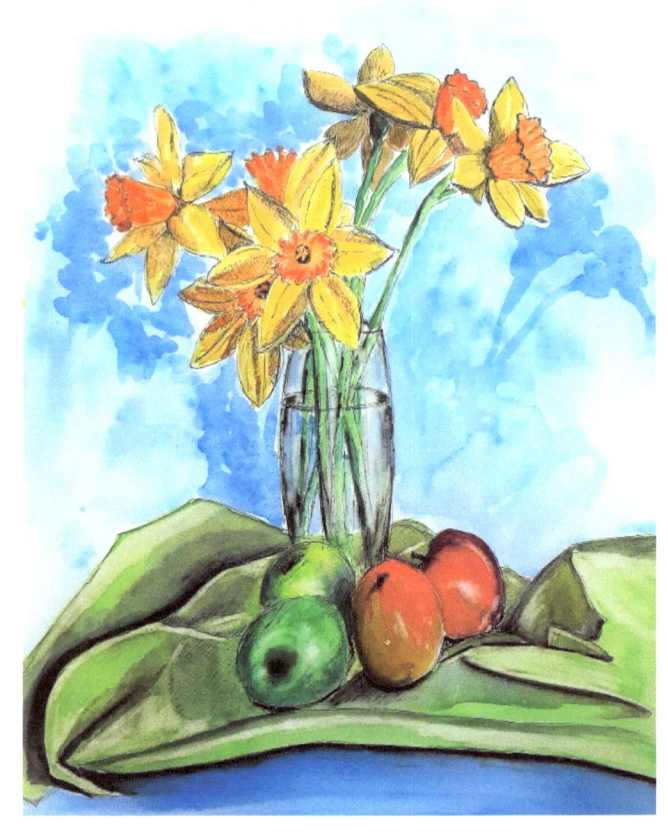

Daffs and apples **Pen and Wash, 2021**

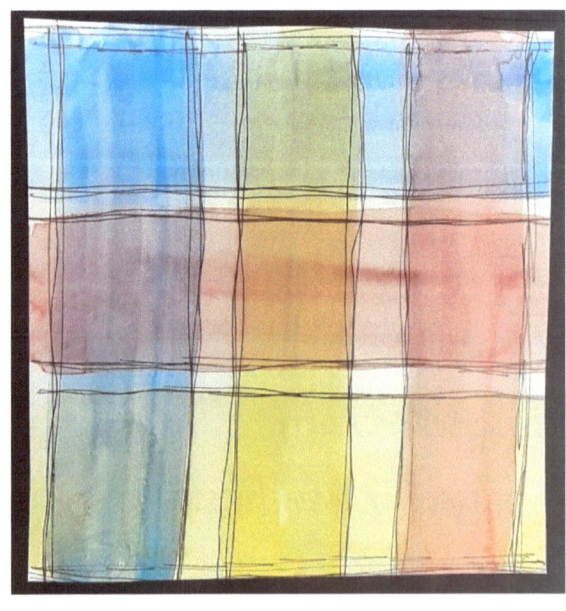

Abstract **Pen and Wash, 2021**

A ten minute experiment in pen and wash abstract.

Painting the dark

Painting the dark can be challenging, but it's so worthwhile for the drama it creates

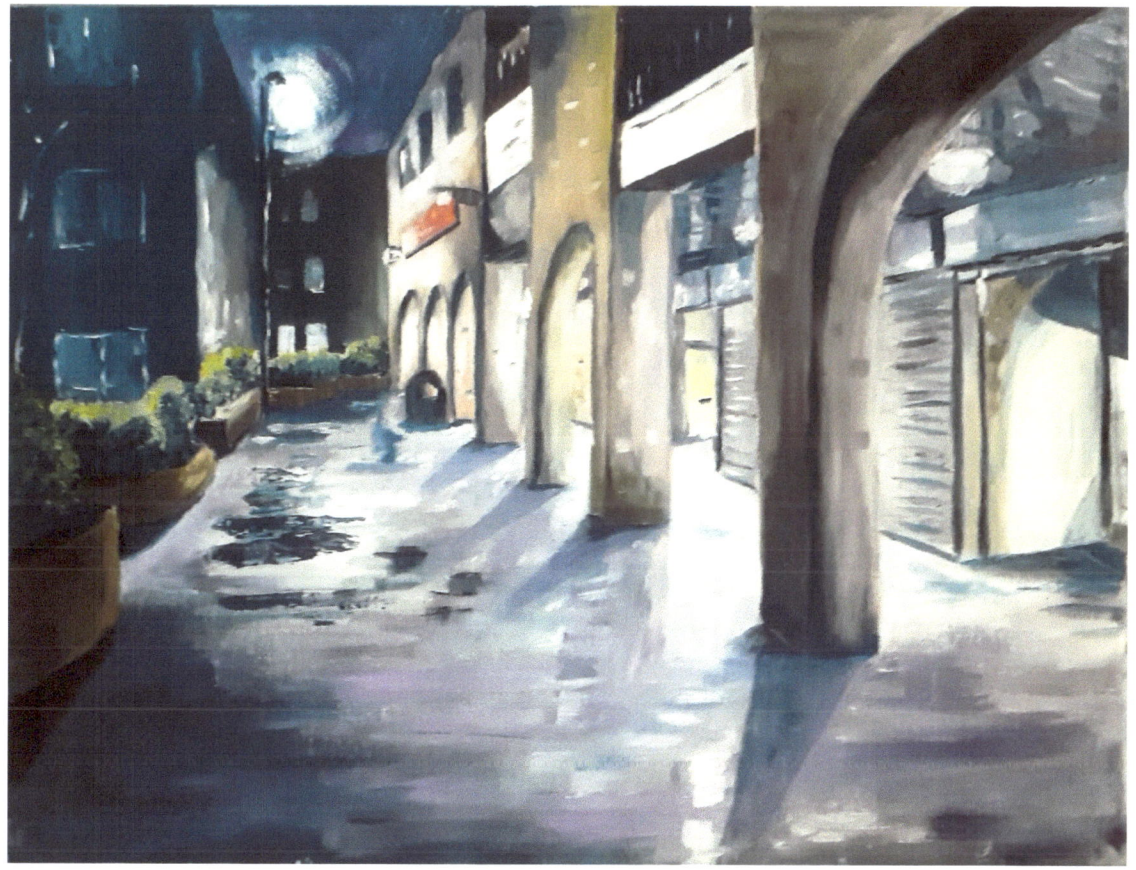

Rickleton Village Centre   Oil on canvas, 16" x 12"

Evening in Rickleton Village, Washington, Tyne & Wear.

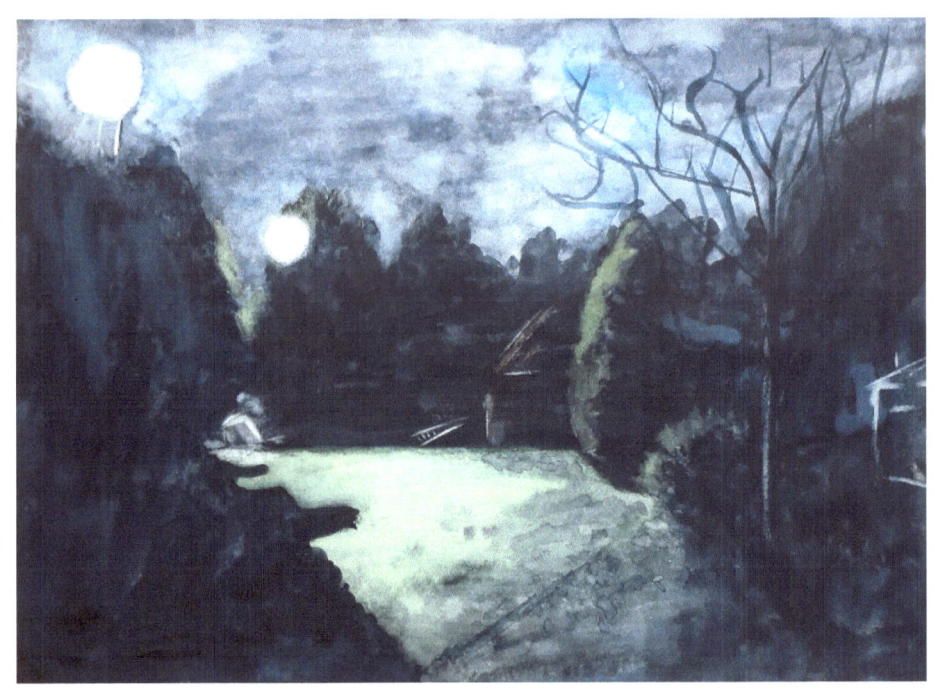

My back garden at night, two different views. Both done in watercolour.

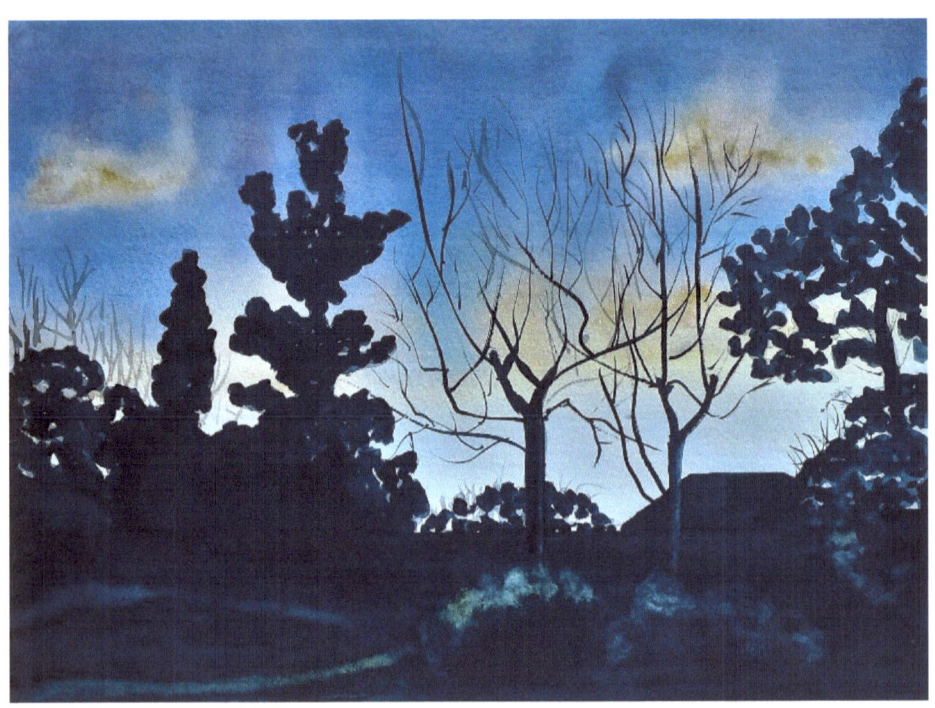

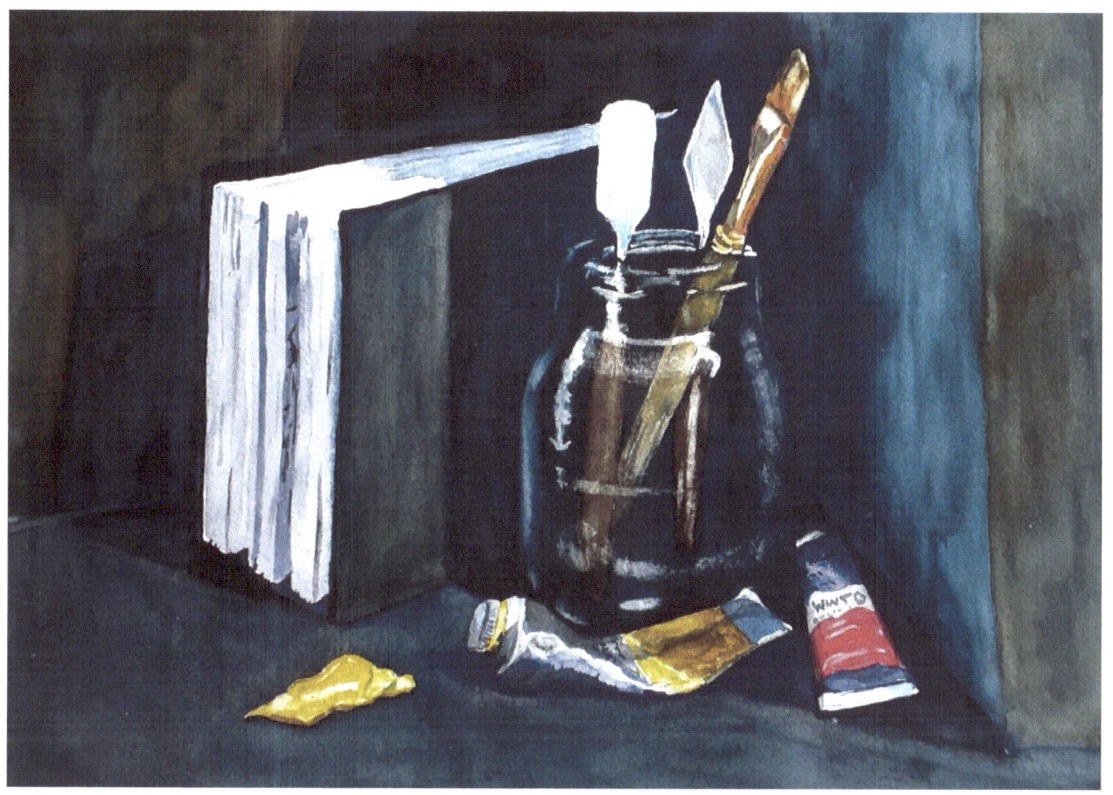

Oils and Water Watercolour, 12" x 16". 2020

During the pandemic lockdown my art classes have carried on but through a zoom class. One of these class tasks was to paint something located in a dark corner. I gave it a twist by depicting oil painting equipment in watercolour, hence the title.

The Landscape

For a long time I was convinced that I would never be able to paint a landscape. Trees seemed beyond me. Until I realised that I didn't have to paint every leaf separately and in perfect form. Now I just have fun with landscape.

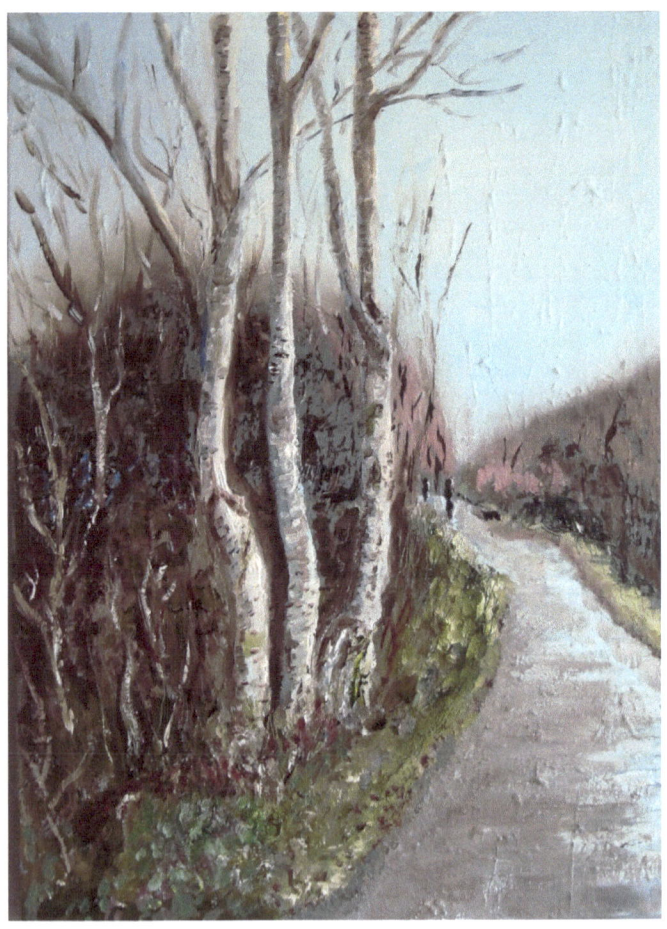

C2C Washington **Oil on Canvas**

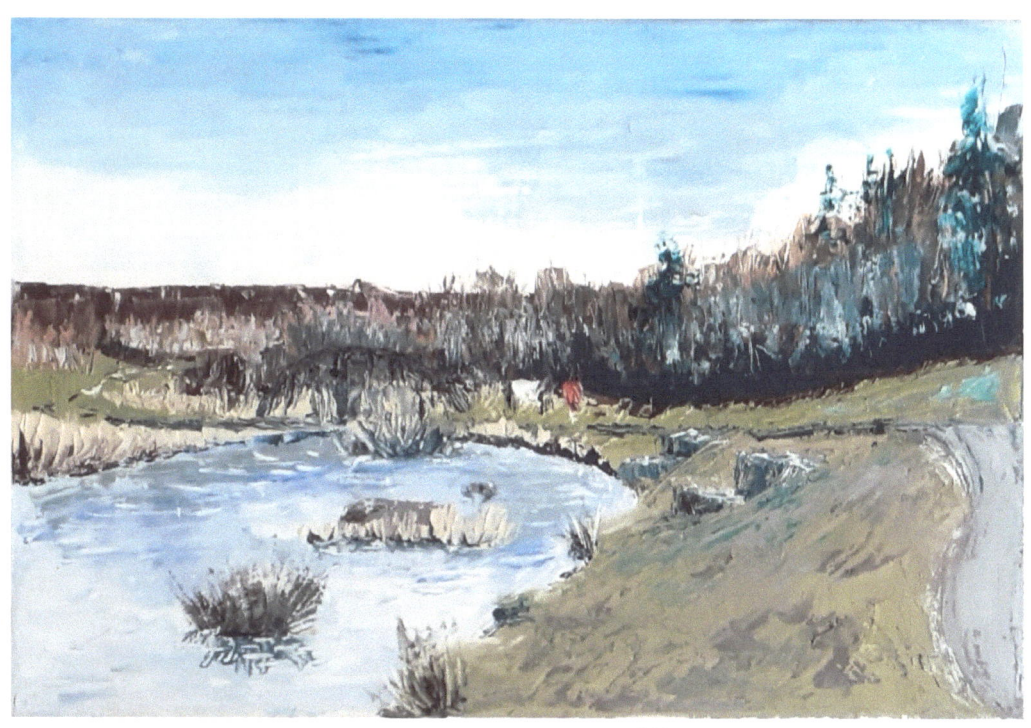

Herrington Park, Tyne & Wear Oil on canvas, 6" x 12". 2020

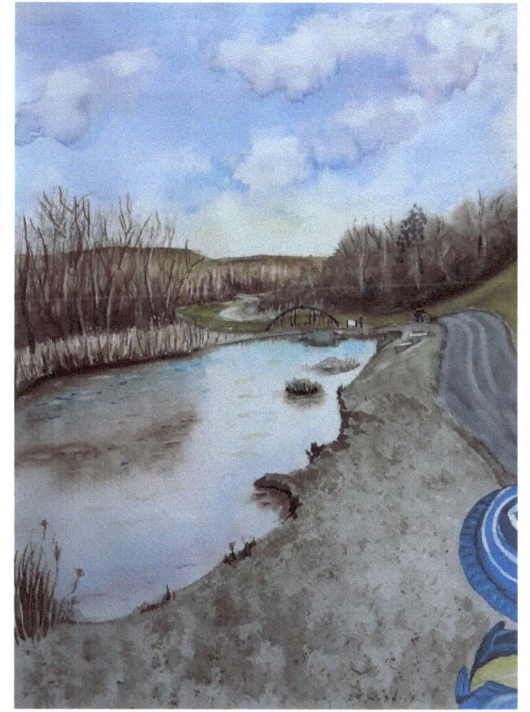

Watercolour. 2020

Both of these paintings are of the same view: Herrington Park which is situated in the North East of England. It's change of use from an open cast mine has been very successful. The oil was done entirely with a pallette knife.

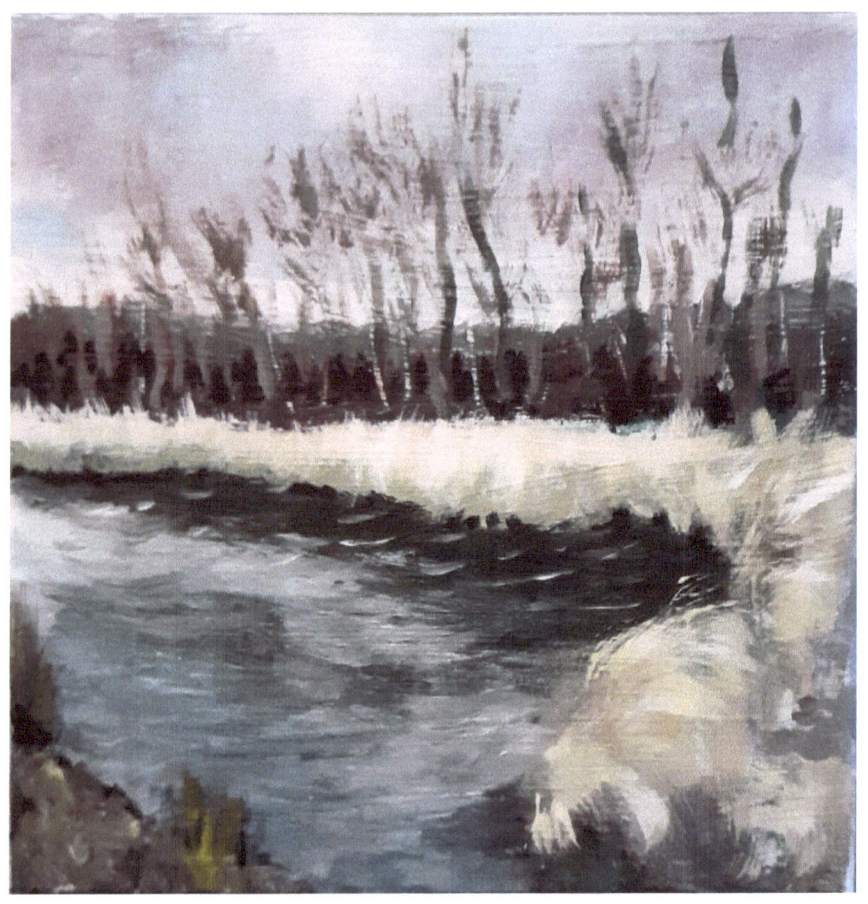

Herrington Park. 2020   **Oil on Canvas. 6" x 6"**

This is the same view of Herrington Park as the previous two paintings but from the opposite direction. It's painted on a tiny canvas and was very quick to do but despite that, I just love it.

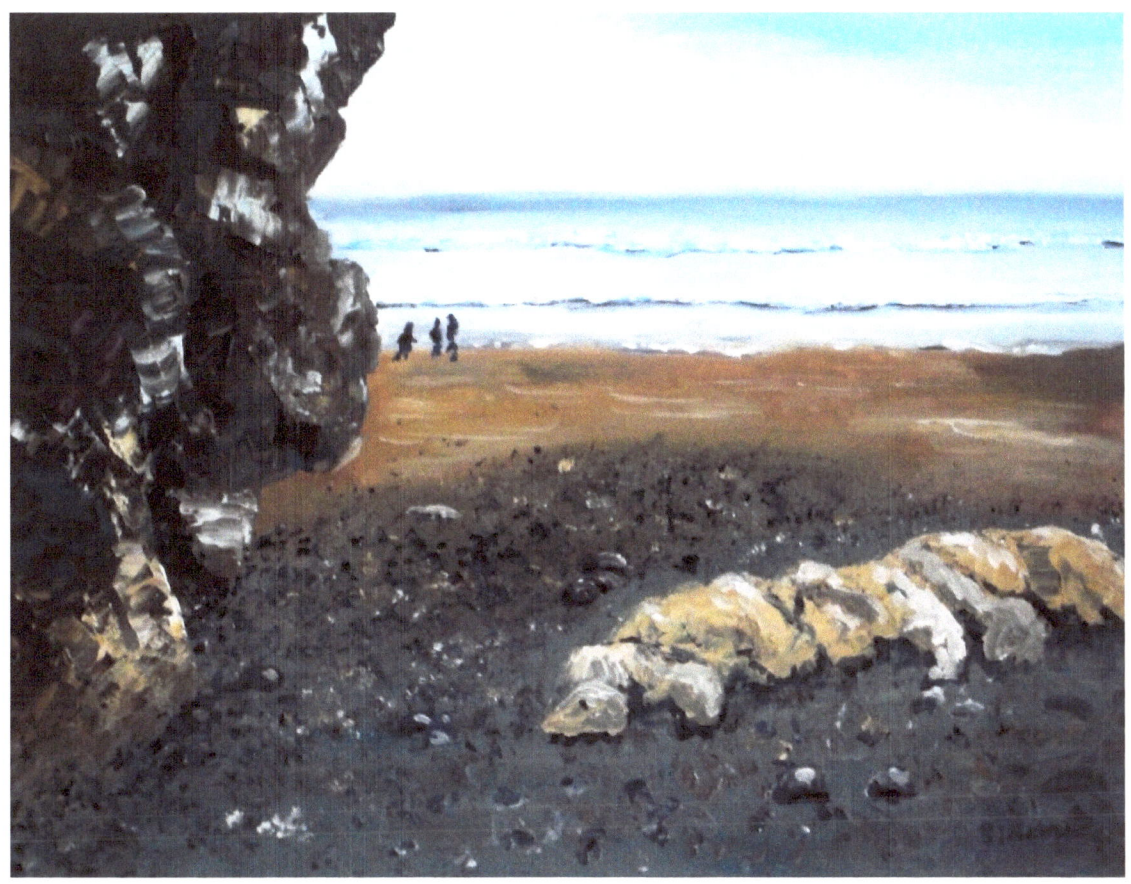

Seaham Beach   Oil on canvas, 12" x 16"

An oil painting of Seaham Beach in Tyne and Wear. I like to come here to walk and look for pieces of sea glass for which the beach is world famous.

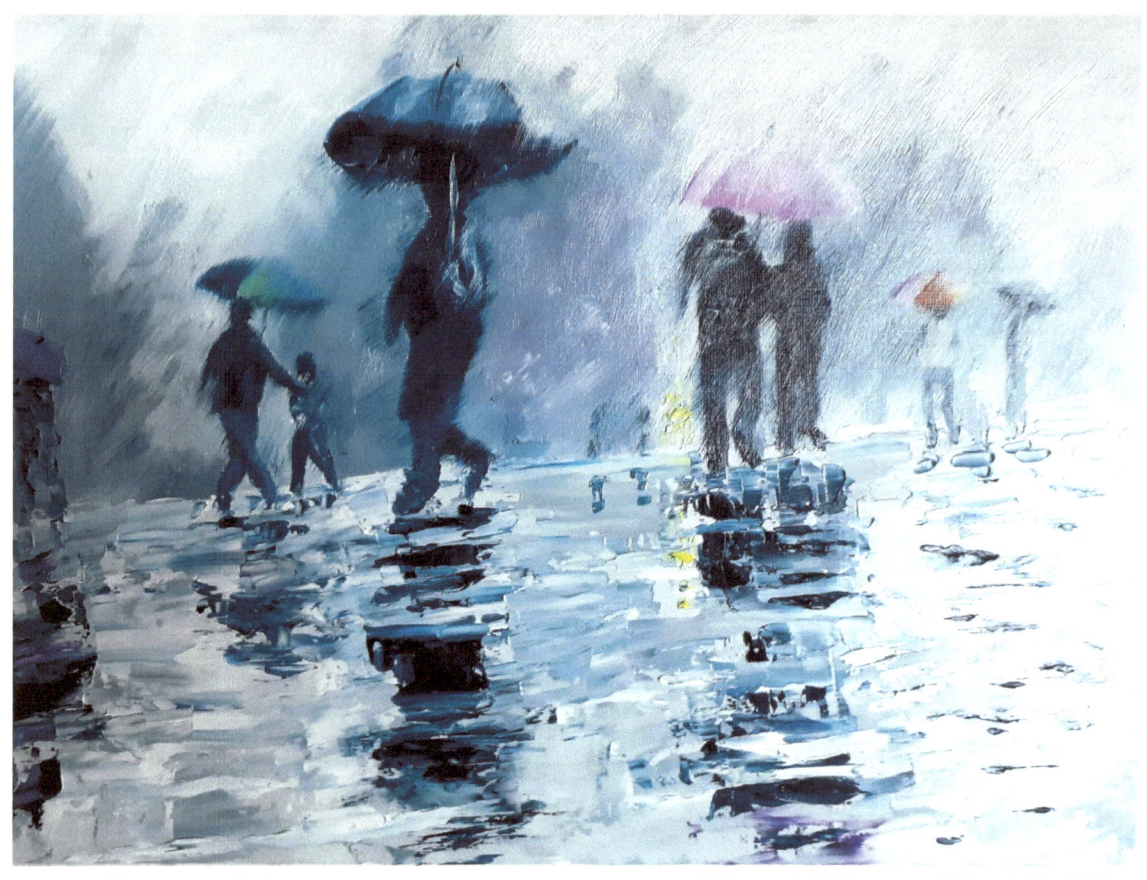

Umbrellas and Rain **Oil on Oil Paper, 12" x 16". 2021**

Painting a rainy landscape, as was the class task, at first seemed impossible, but, after reminding myself that it was only paper and paint I 'roughed up' the painting that I had meticulously worked on and used a palette knife to good effect to create the impression of rain. I think it worked.

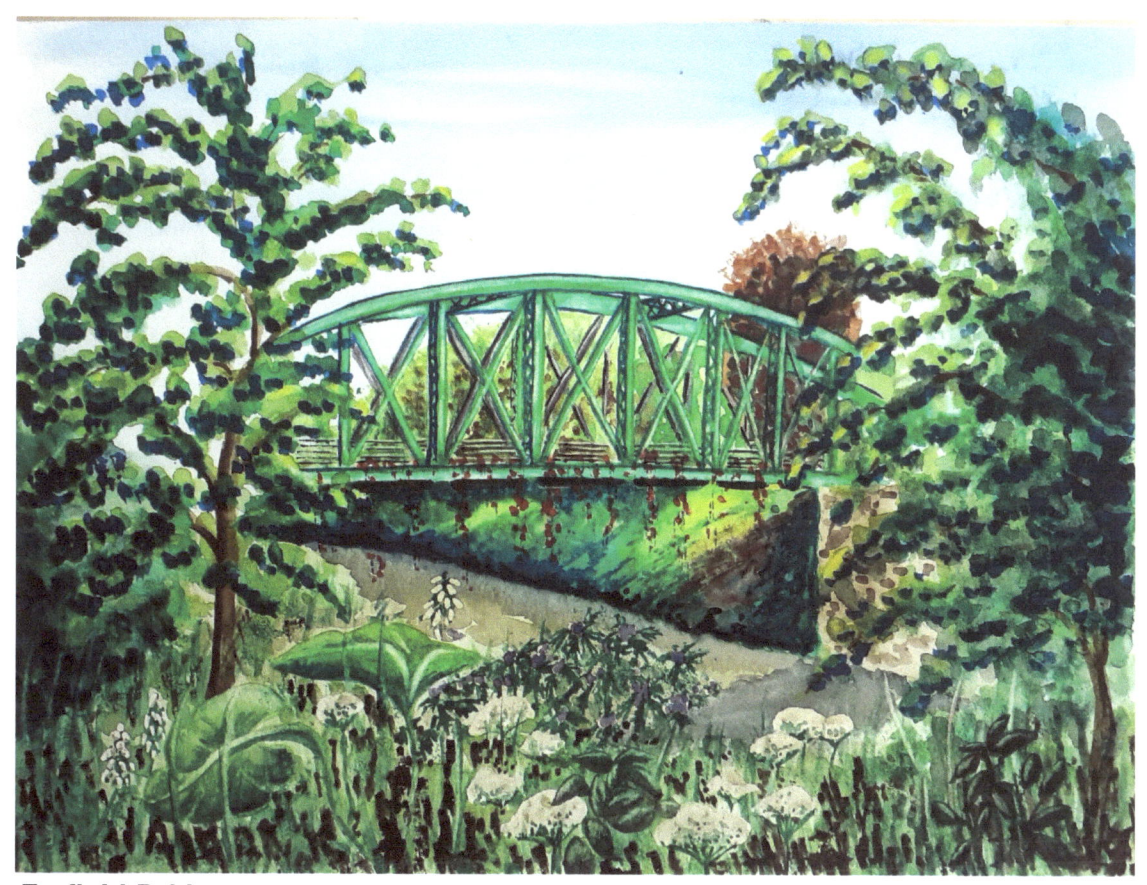

Fatfield Bridge   **Watercolour**

Fatfield Bridge crosses the River Wear at Fatfield, Washington, Tyne & Wear in the North East of England. This tight little watercolour was painted on a sunny afternoon on one of the class's rare field trips. What a lovely day that was.

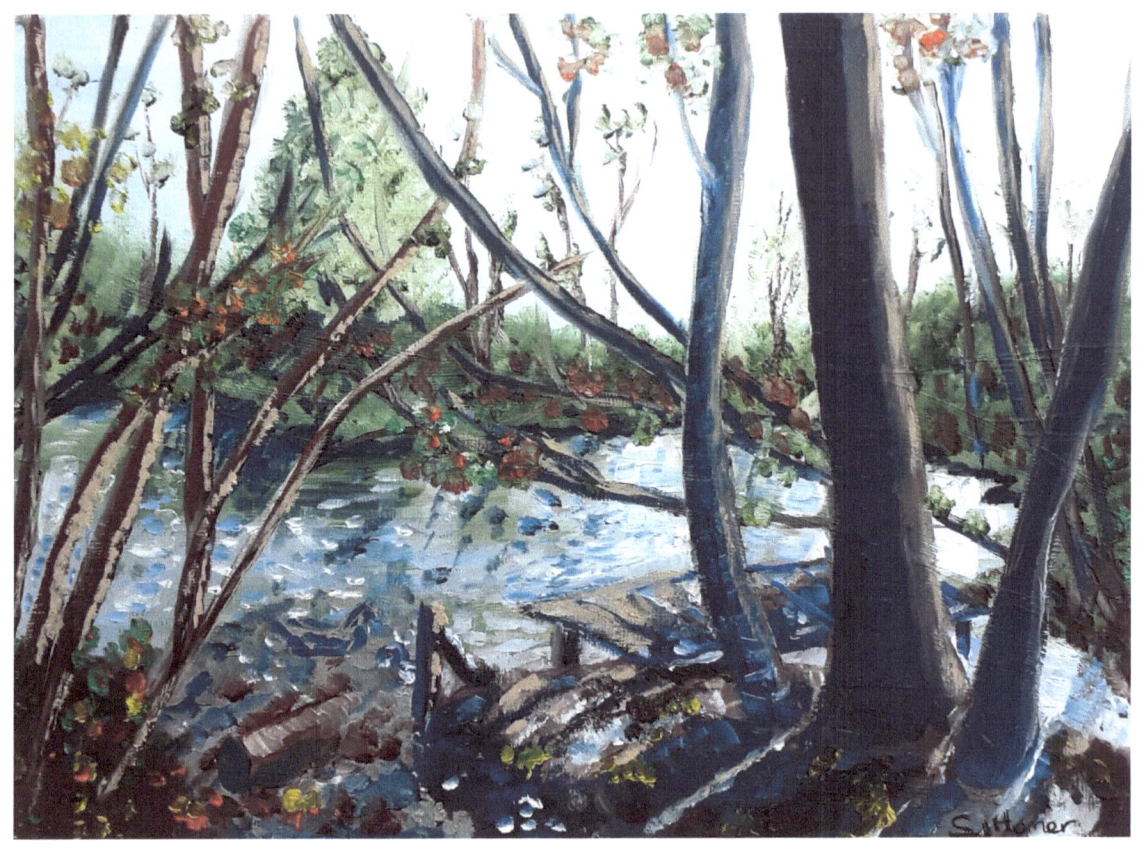

Rickleton Duck Pond, 2021 Oil on Oil paper, A4

Rickleton duck pond resides in a tiny woodland situated in the centre of the residential area of Rickleton, Washington. It has been a regular route for my daily walk during the covid 19 lockdown and is a little gem amongst buildings where many, many ducks frequent. If you look carefully you can see one of those ducks in my painting.

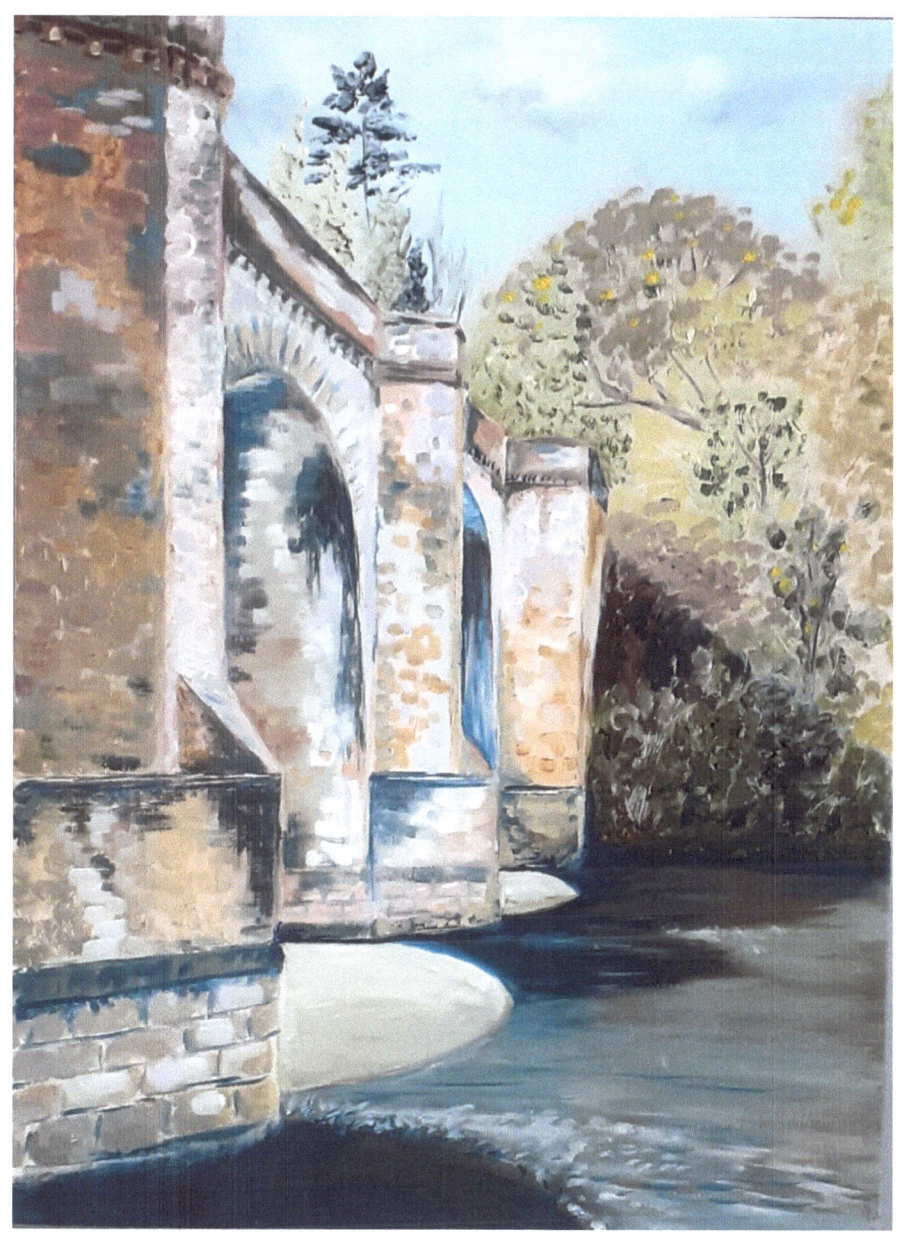

A Bridge in Durham Oil on Canvas, 12" x 16"

A bridge on the River Wear close to Durham Cathedral.

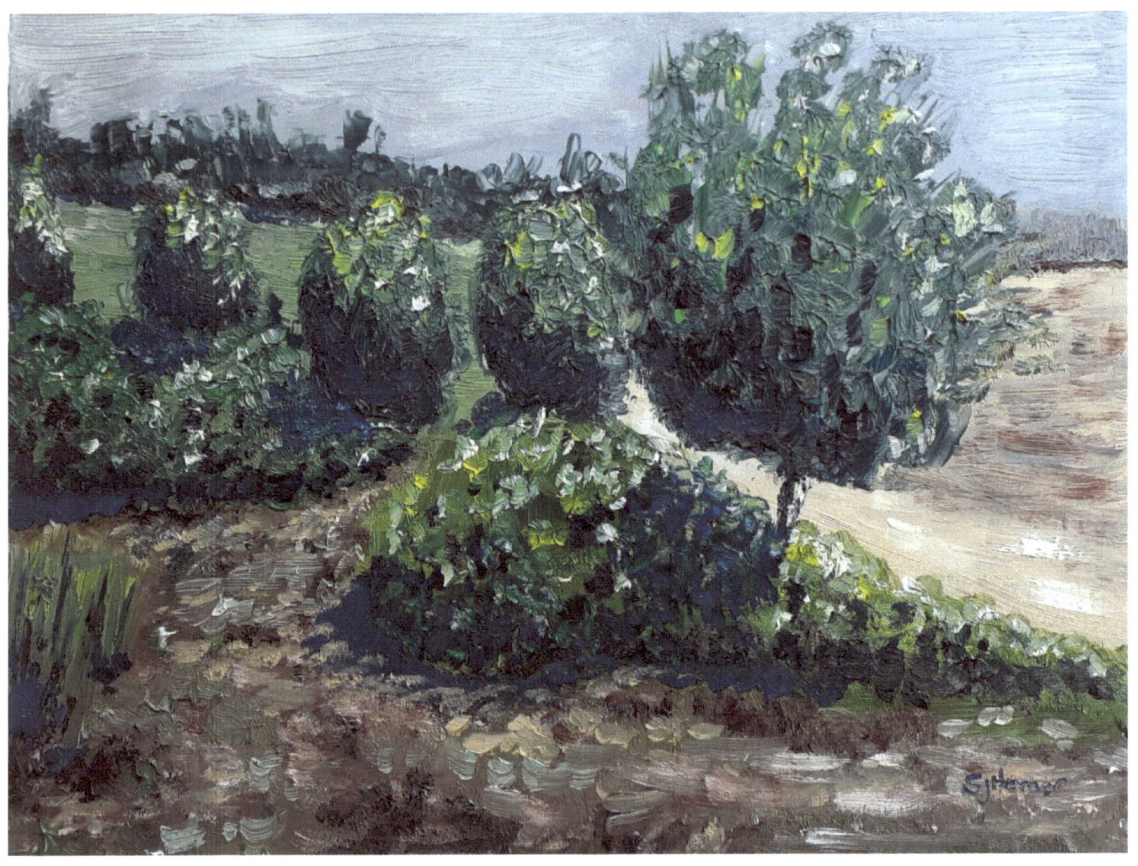

Derwent Water   Oil on Oil Paper, 12" x 16"

A trip to Derwent Water is the subject of this loosely painted oil. It features not the water but the surrounding greenery.

Somewhere amongst those shrubs my grandchildren are hiding waiting to jump out on me.

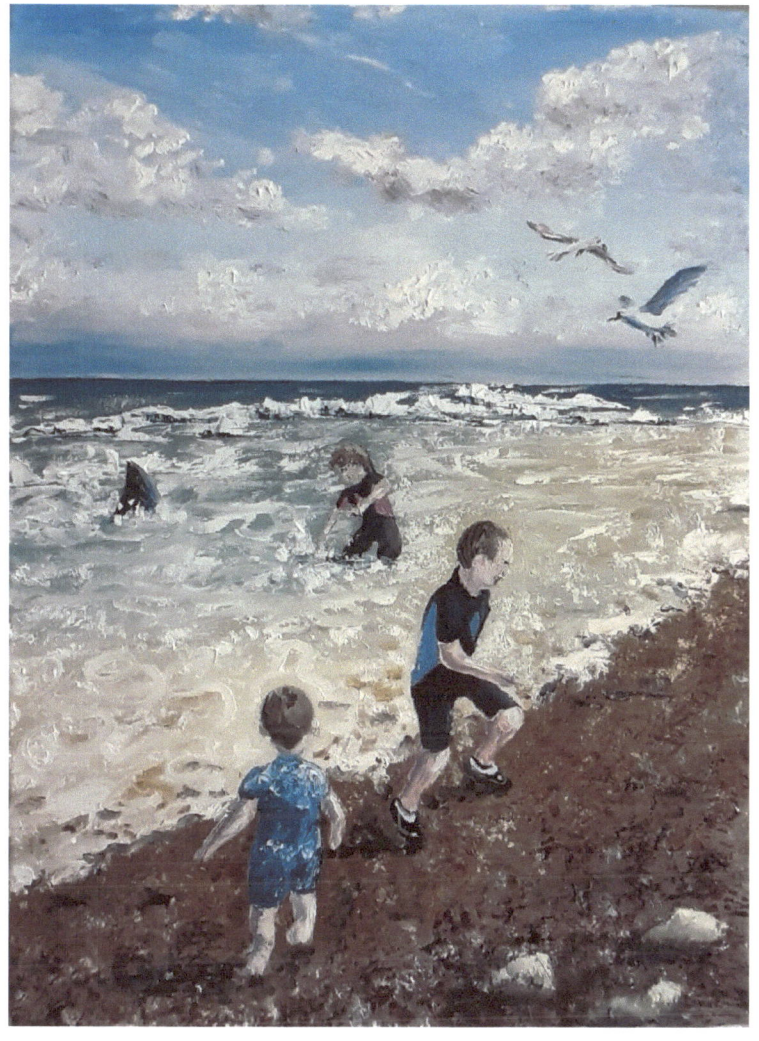

Cromer 2020 Oil on Canvas, 12" x 16"

An exercise in pathways through the painting.

This was taken from a photo of my grandchilden Tommy, Liam, Finn, Albie and Emma on a camping holiday in Cromer, Norfolk. The baby twins, Albie and Emma are symbolised by the seagulls as they were too young to play in the sea. I added the shark just for 'fun' as that was the mood I was in.

Buildings & landmarks

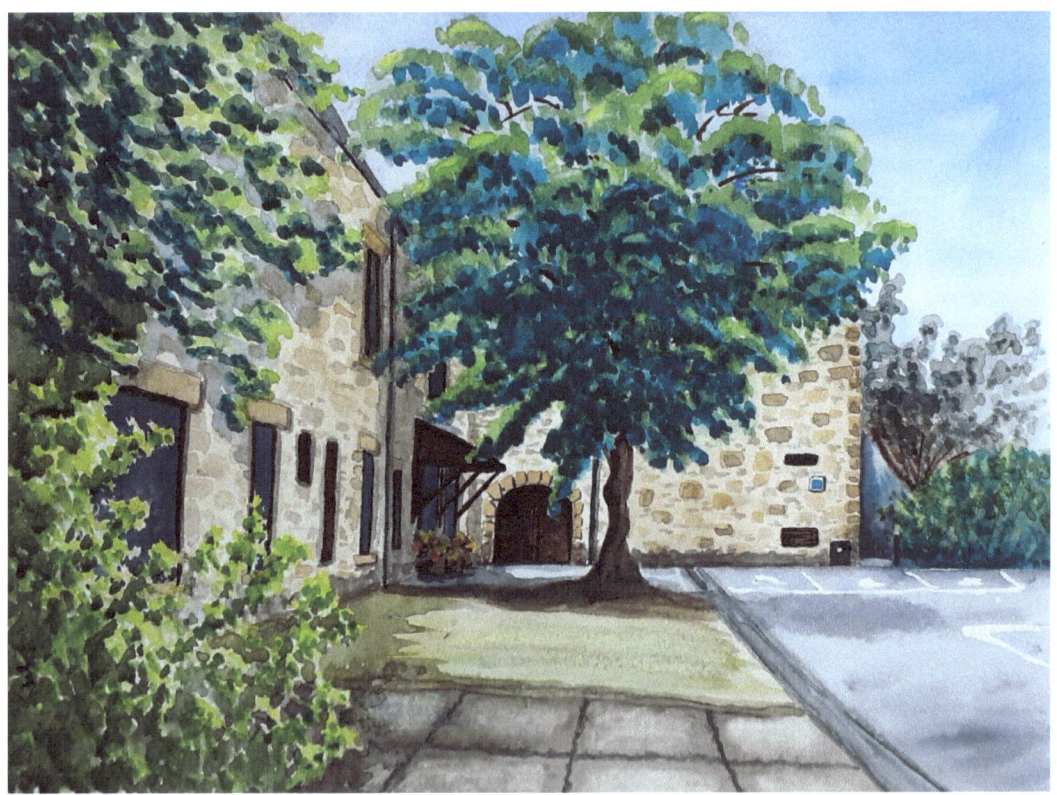

Arts Centre Washington   **Watercolour**

This is where my painting journey began and continues. The Arts Centre Washington. I have plenty of paintings of this and the surrounding buildings as when it's sunny we sometimes have our class outside.

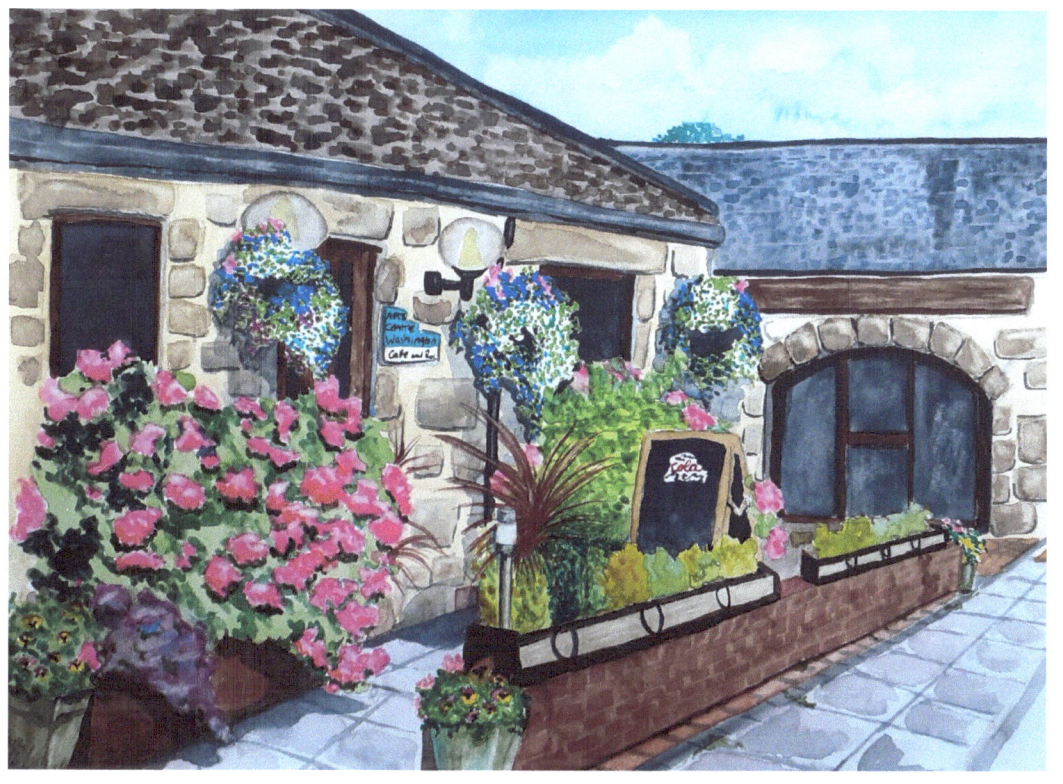

The Courtyard   **Watercolour**

The Courtyard Cafe is situated at the back of the Arts Centre Washington and is a great place to get coffee or lunch and socialise with the rest of the group or meet someone who doesn't attend the class.

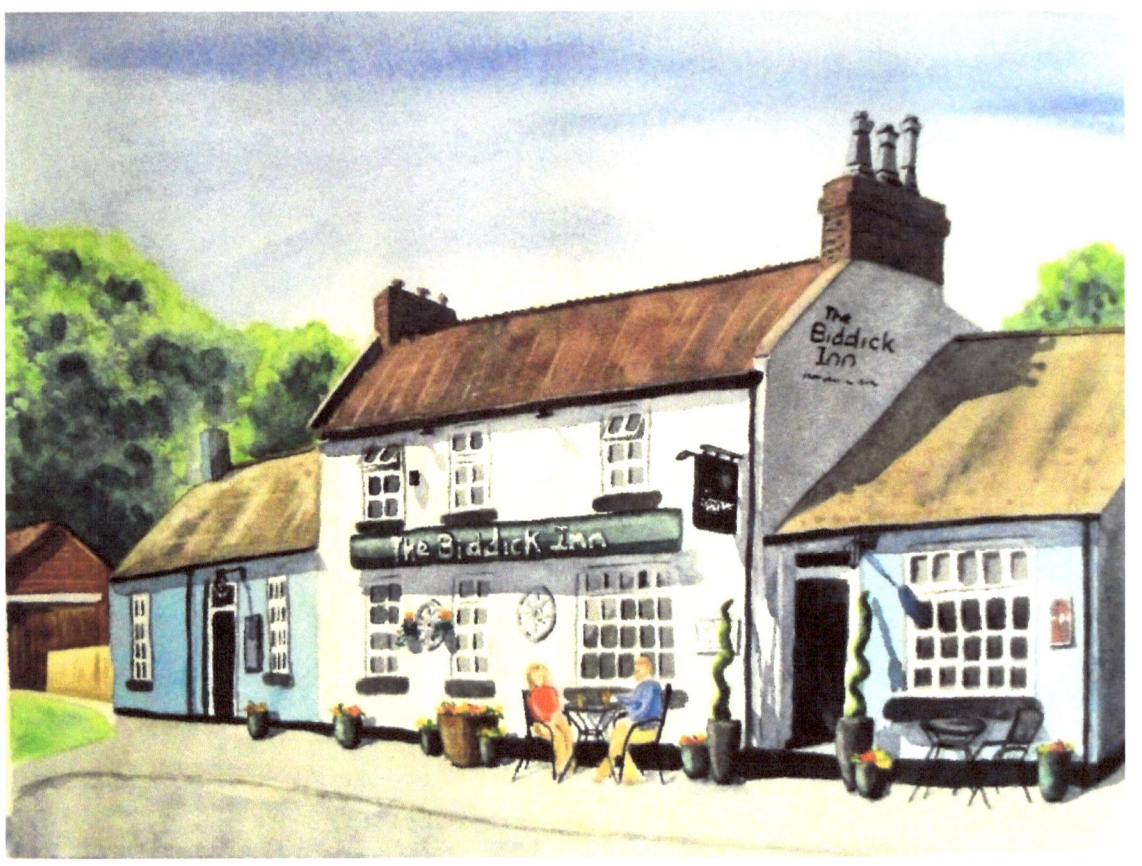

The Biddick Inn   Watercolour, 12" x 16"

The Biddick Inn stands on the other side of the road to Fatfield Bridge that crosses over the River Wear. This watercolour was painted on another one of our class field trips.

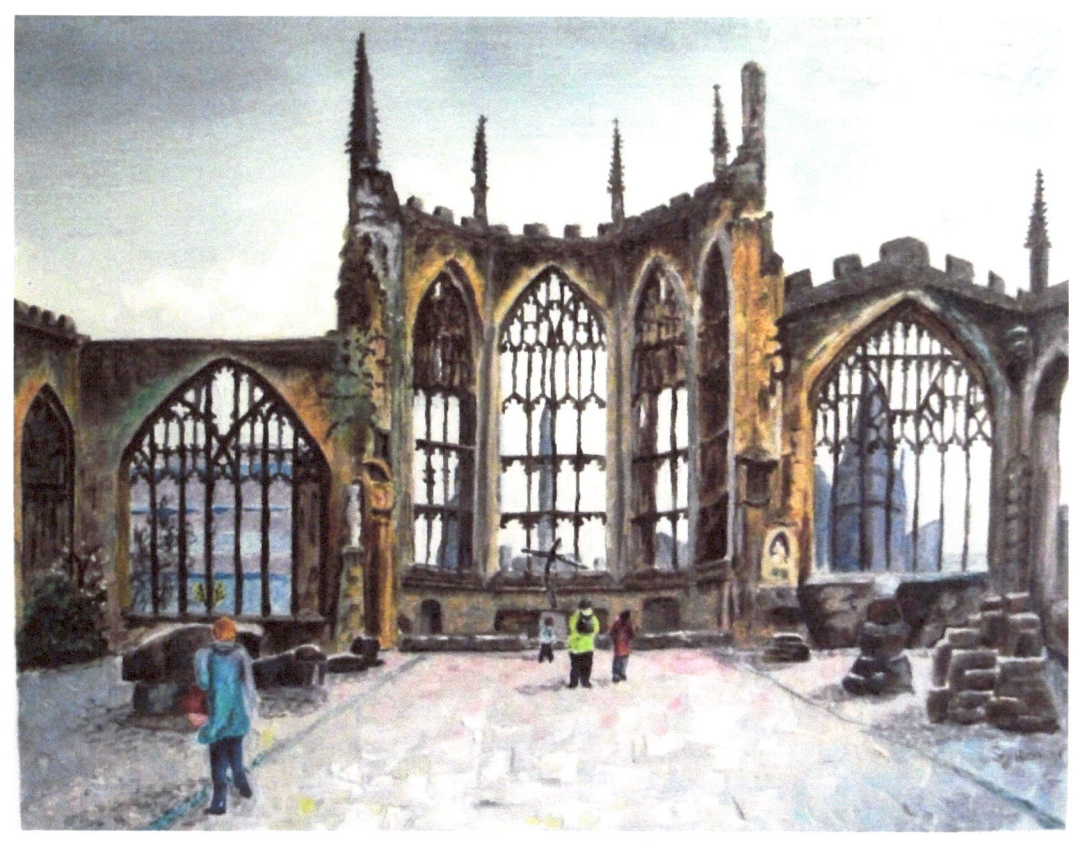

Coventry Old Cathedral   Oil on Canvas Paper, 12" x 16"

I couldn't possibly have a building section without including an oil painting of Coventry's old Cathedral as Coventry is my hometown. Coventry Cathedral was destroyed during the blitz of 1940. The cross in the middle of the ruin was formed by two massive nails welding themselves together during the intense heat. There is now a 'new' Cathedral built next to the ruined one.

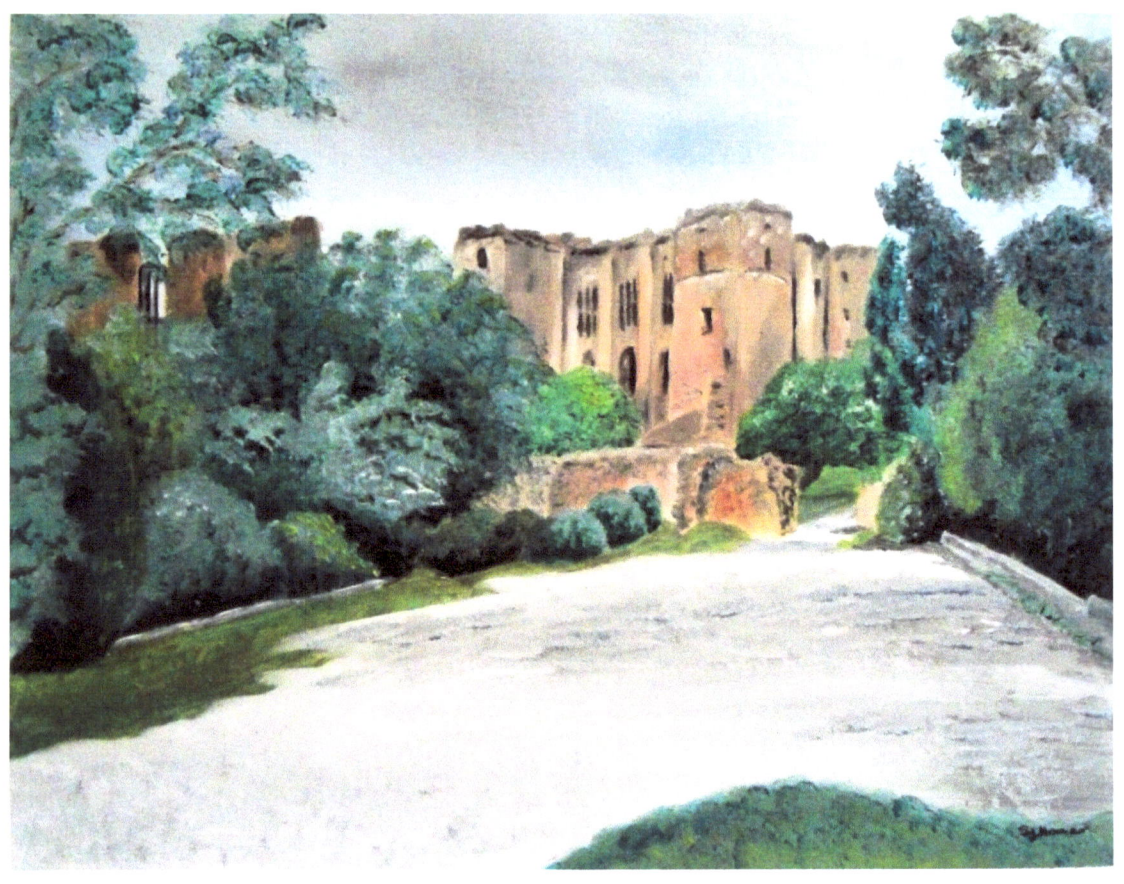

Kenilworth Castle Oil on Canvas, 12" x 16"

Although Kenilworth Castle is a ruin, It is now owned by English Heritage and many people visit every year. Cycling past it one day while on holiday in the area, I couldn't resist taking photo's and later turned those photo's into this oil painting.

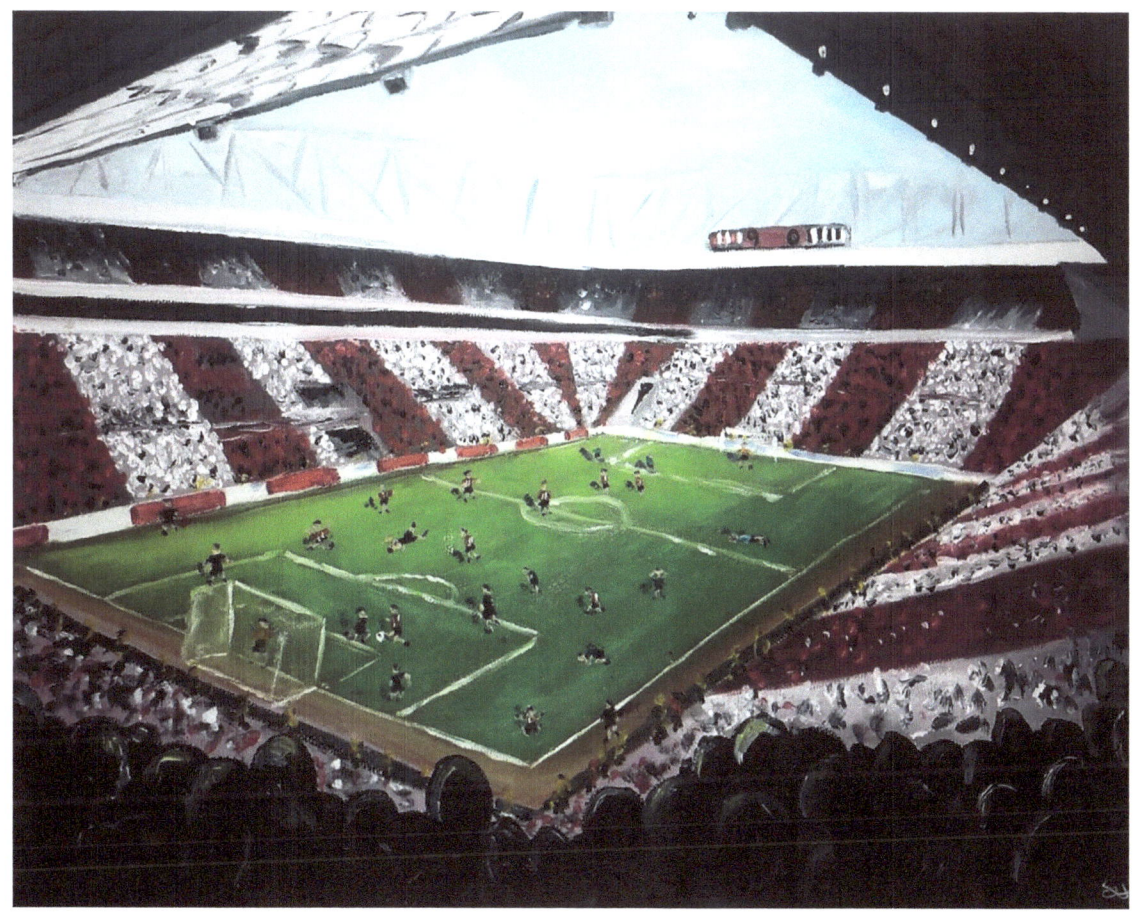

Sunderland AFC   **Oil on Canvas**

This was a birthday gift for my Sunderland Football Club mad grandson, Liam. He loved it.

Wildlife

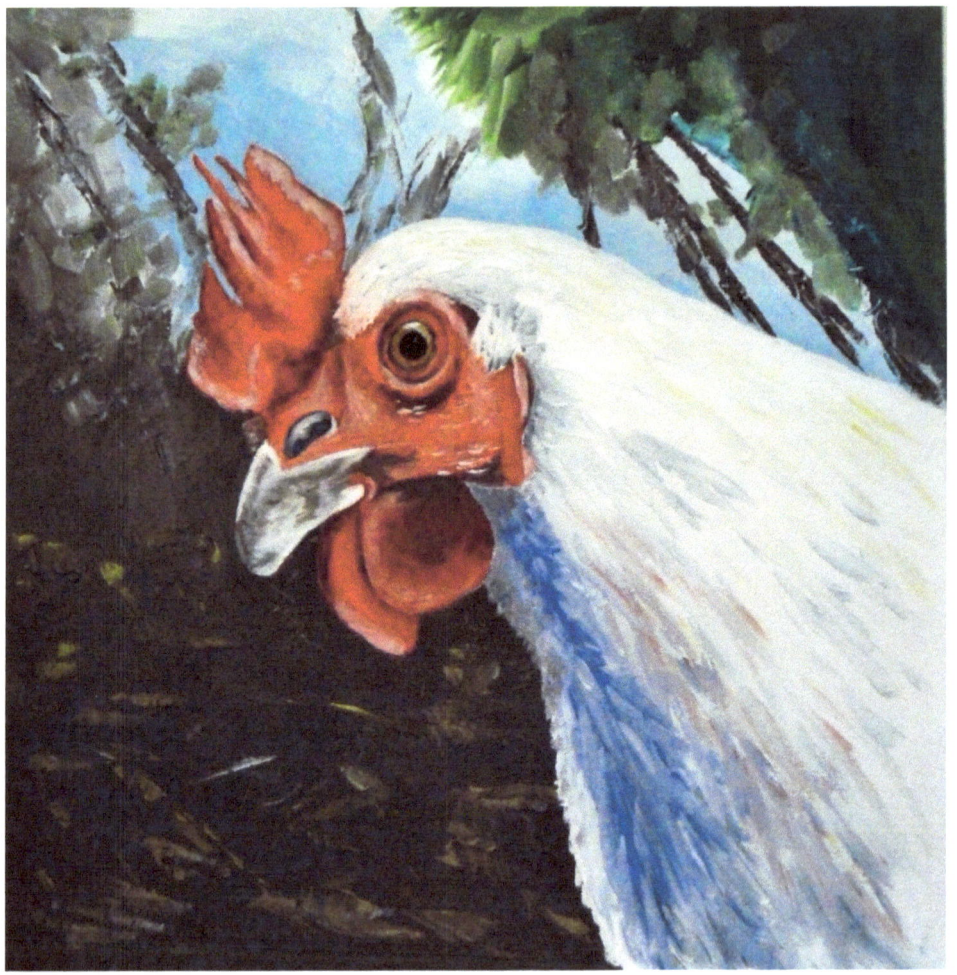

Layla   Oil on Canvas, 12" x 12"

Layla was one of our pet chickens, she had the sweetest, friendliest nature and would hop onto your lap to be petted like a cat.

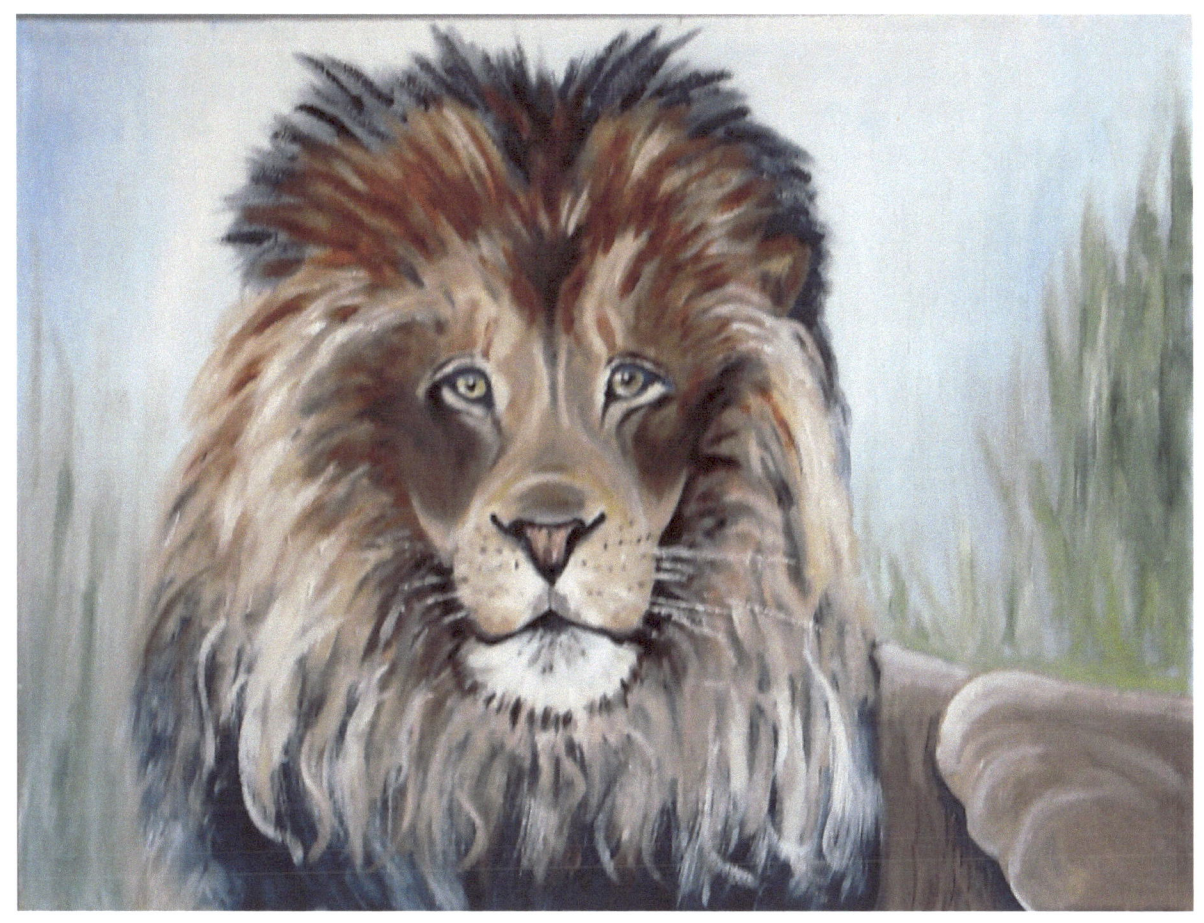

Wild Thing   **Oil on Canvas, 12" x 16"**

This oil painting of a magnificent male lion was done from a photograph which I obtained from the internet, copyright free of course.

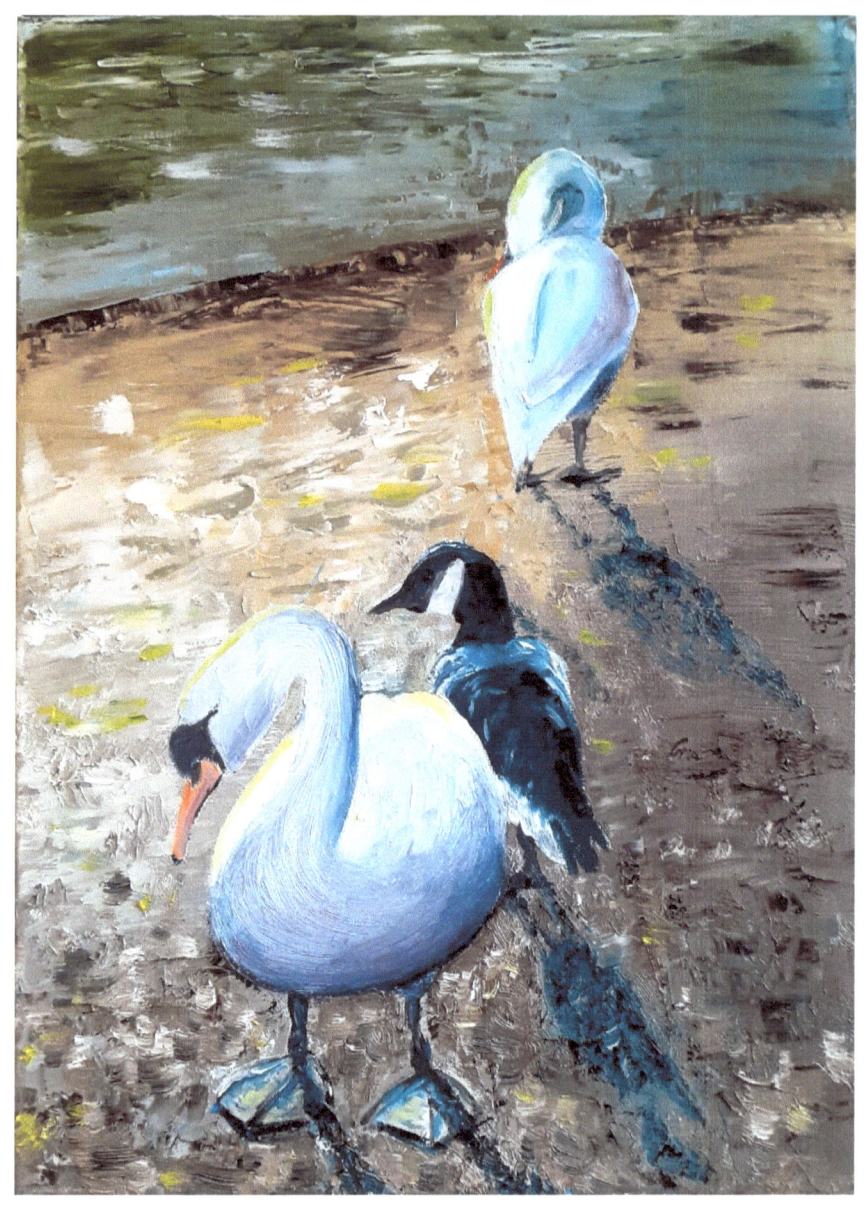

Swans in Herrington Park   Oil on Canvas, 16" x 12"

I absolutely love the light that I managed to capture on this oil painting of some swans in Herrington Park in the North East of England.

People

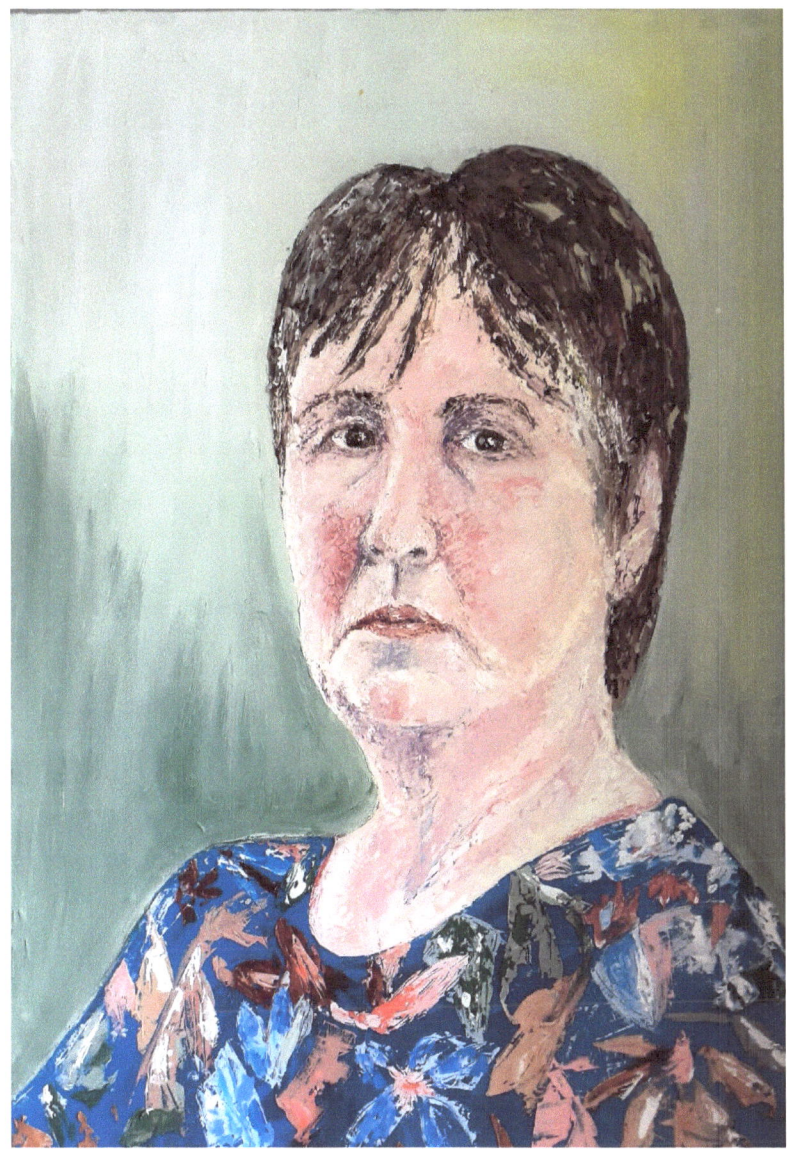

Sandra, A Self Portrait Oil on Canvas. A2

A self portrait done with a palette knife. I'm not miserable, I'm a very happy person, this is just my concentration face.

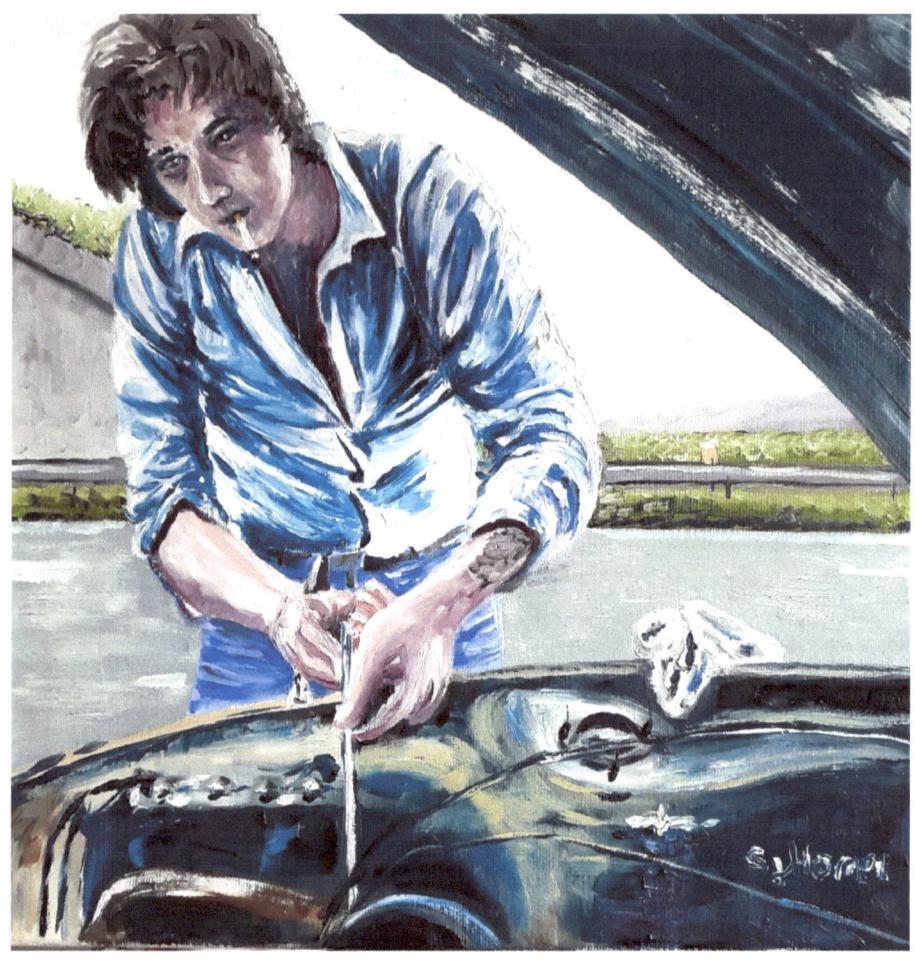

Honeymoon Mechanic   Oil on Canvas, 12" x 12"

The brief for this painting was 'an incident' I looked through old photo's and found my subject. This is my brother Alan, aged 20 on the way back from his honeymoon in the Scottish Highlands in 1980. They broke down. Good job he was a car mechanic at the time.

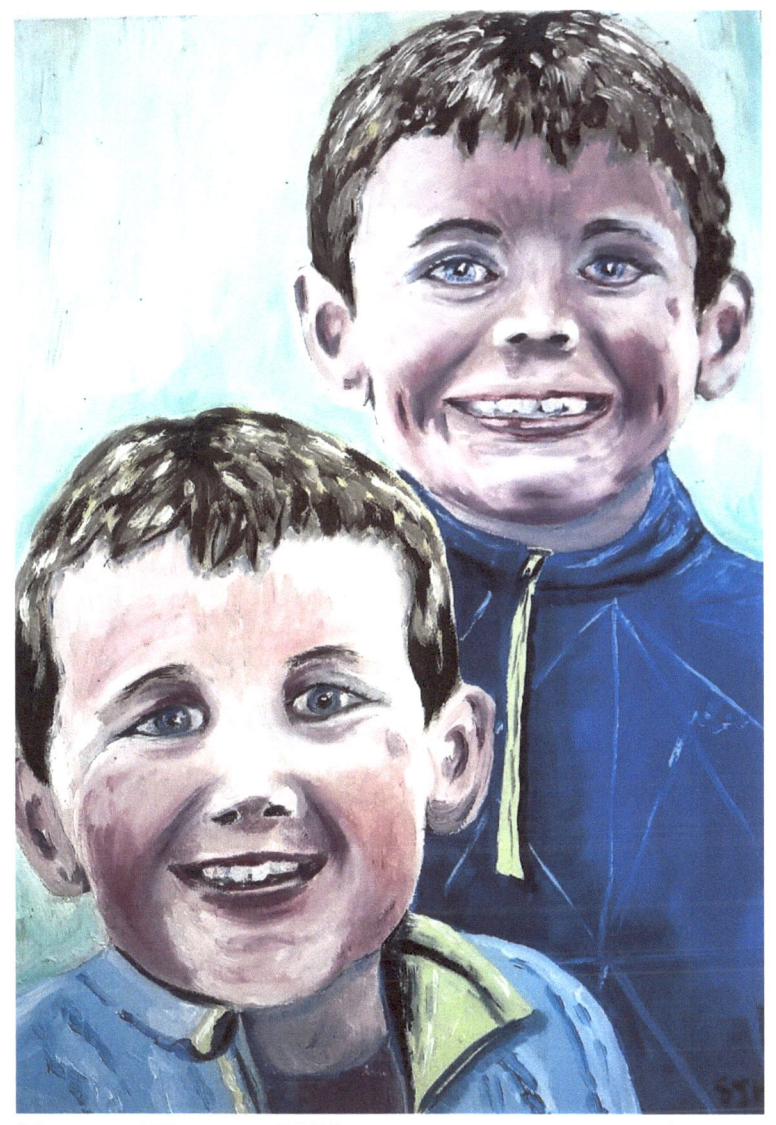

Liam and Tommy. 2020 **Oil on Canvas**

One of my first portraits. My two eldest grandsons, Tommy and Liam. I did this as a gift for my daughter Cathy's birthday when we were in lockdown and I couldn't get out to buy her something.

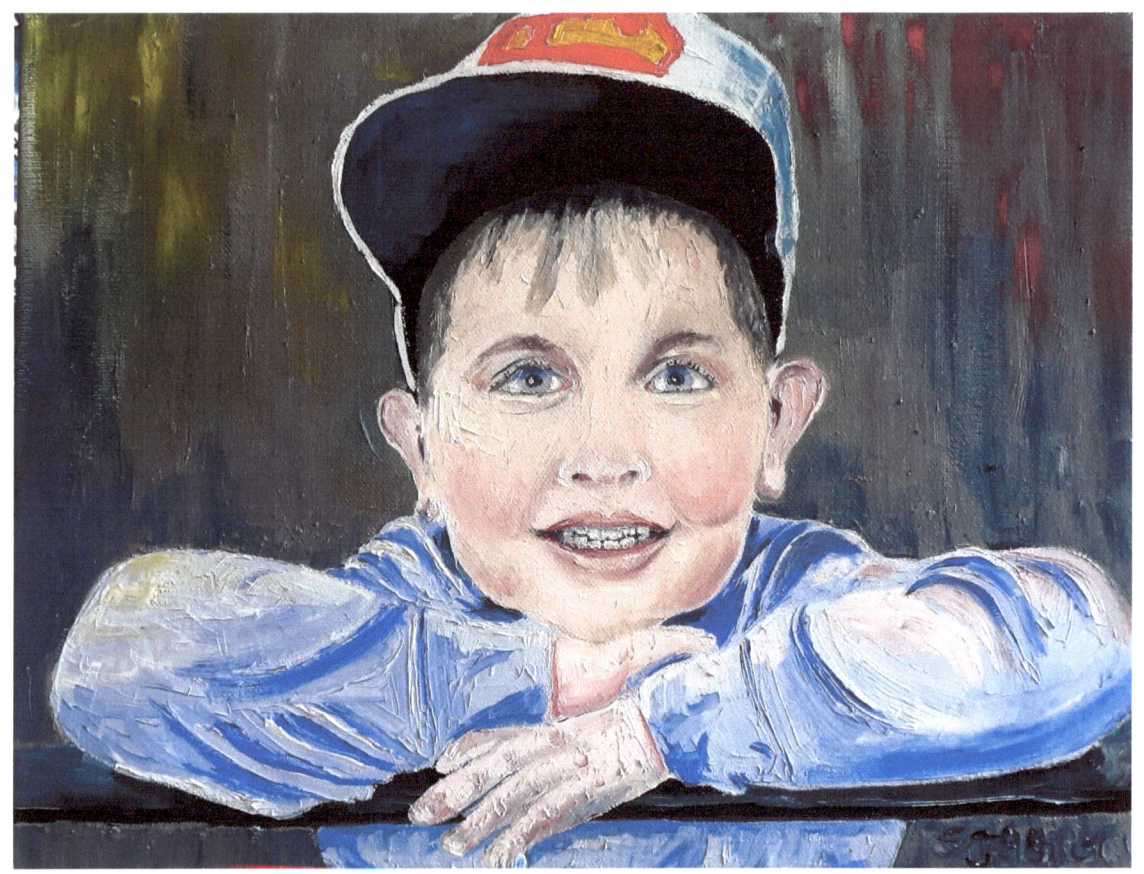

Finn Oil on Canvas, 12" x 16"

My older daughter and her family don't live near to me and I miss them so much. So when I got this lovely photo of Finn, my grandson, I just had to put it on canvas.

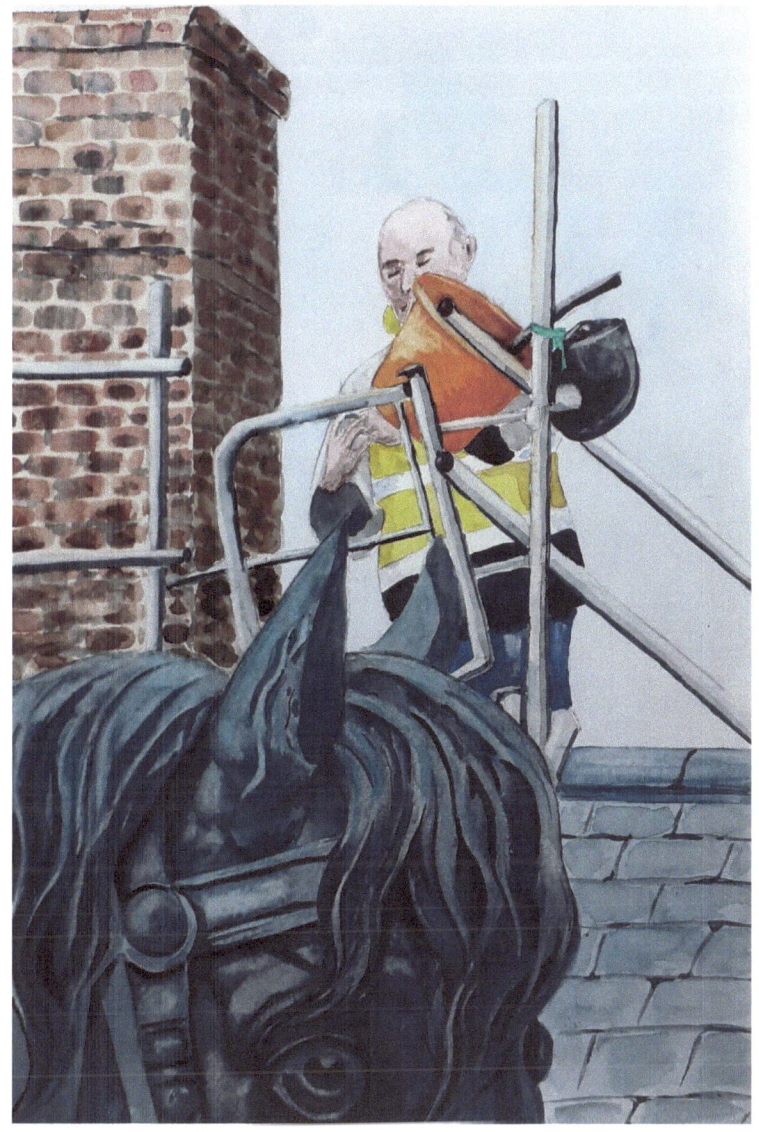

Man at Work   **Watercolour**

A man at work on a rooftop in Durham City Centre. I used some artistic licence to move the image of the statue because I wanted it in the picture.

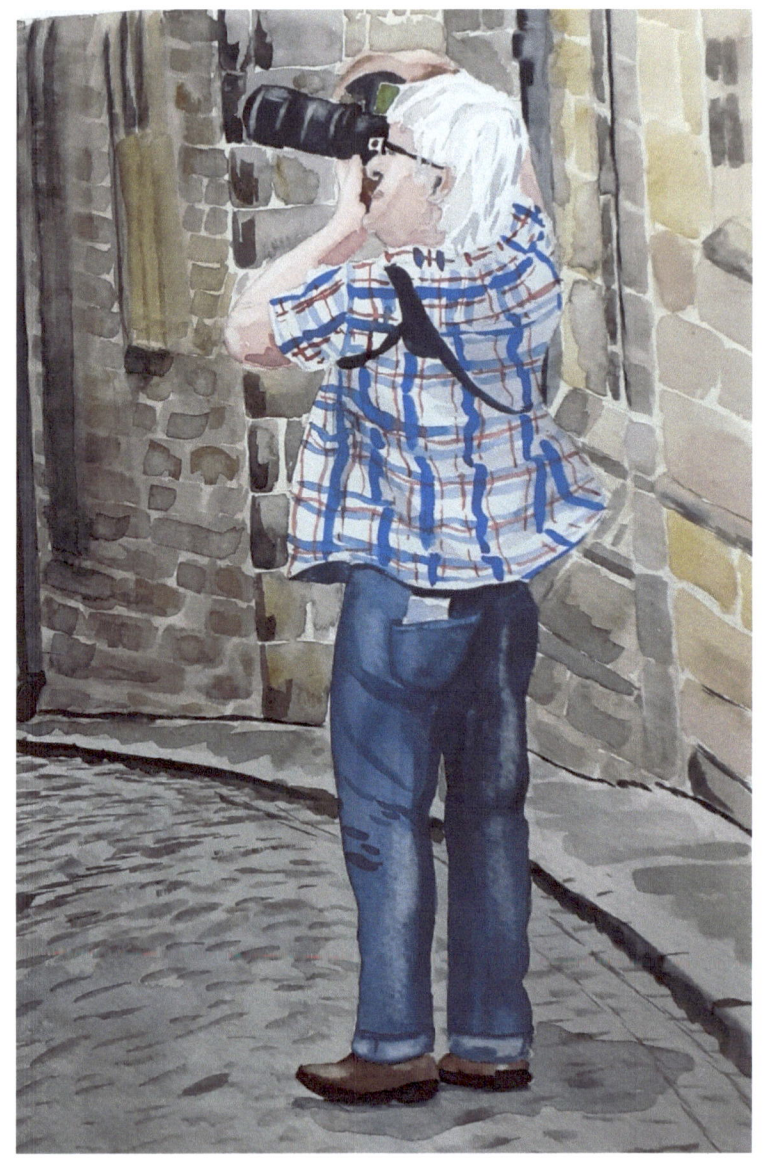

The photographer   **Watercolour**

A man taking a photograph in Durham City Centre. I don't know this man, he was randomly in the background of a photo taken of something else.

Exploring Styles

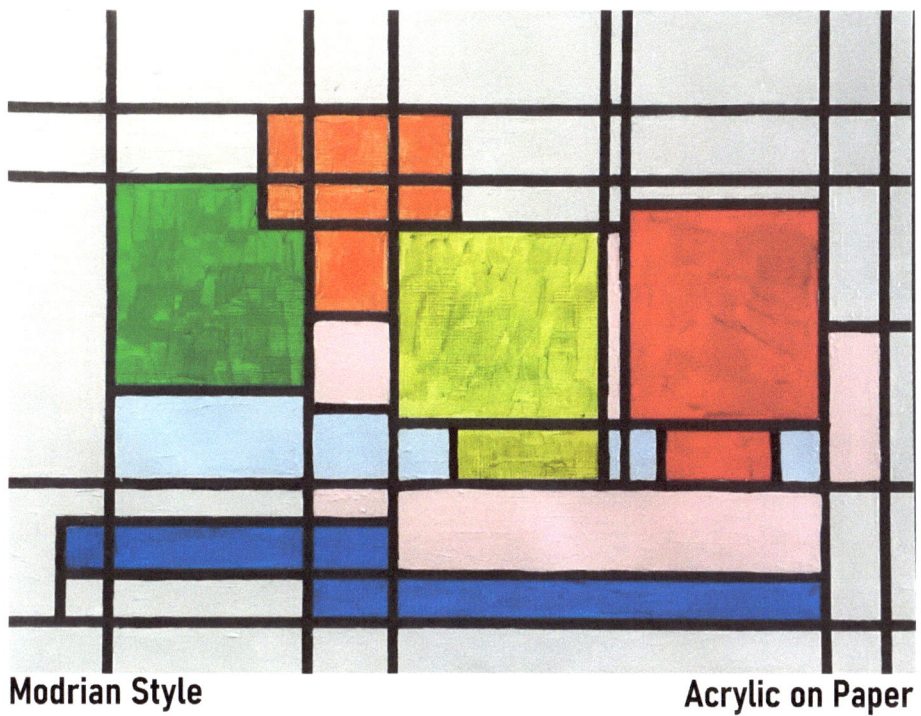

Modrian Style **Acrylic on Paper**

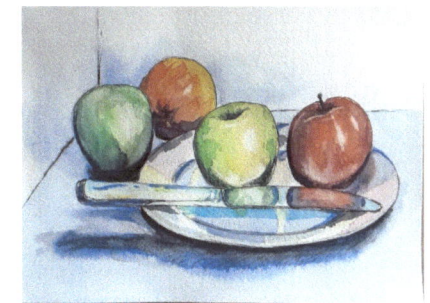

During our lockdown zoom classes we have dipped a toe into the world of modern and abstract art.

The brief for this painting was to use a piece of our own artwork and create a Mondrian style painting. I used my apples and plate watercolour.

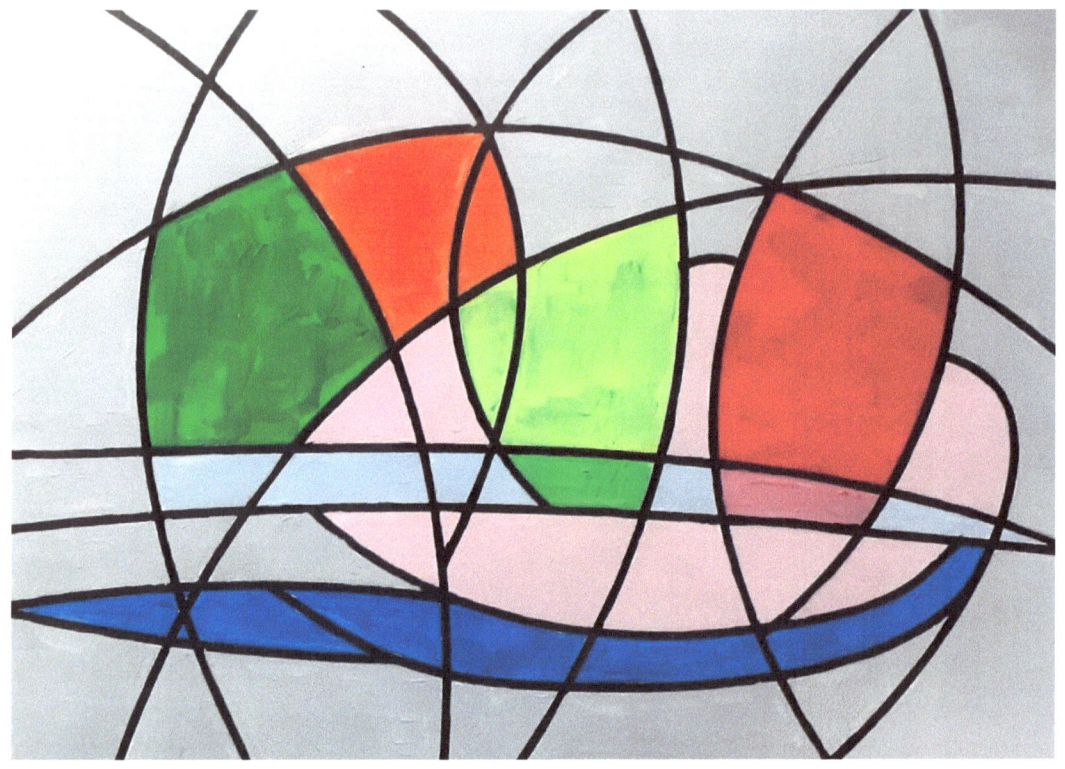

Curvy Mondrian Style **Acrylic on Paper**

I don't pretend to fully understand this style of painting but it was a lot of fun to do so I decided to use the same source material to create a curvy example.

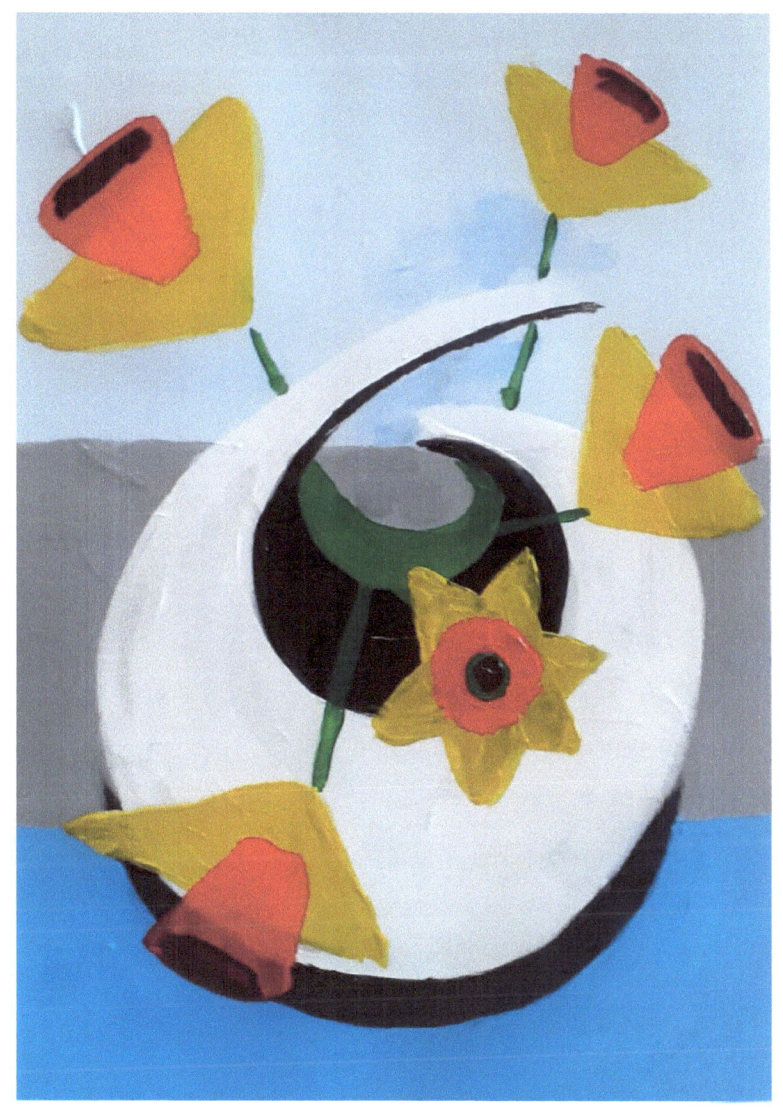

Daffodil Creation   **Acrylic on Paper**

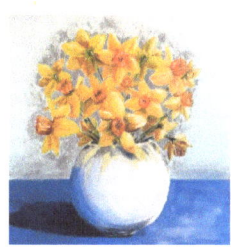

Still having fun, I had a go at exploring a different style for my Happy Daffs.

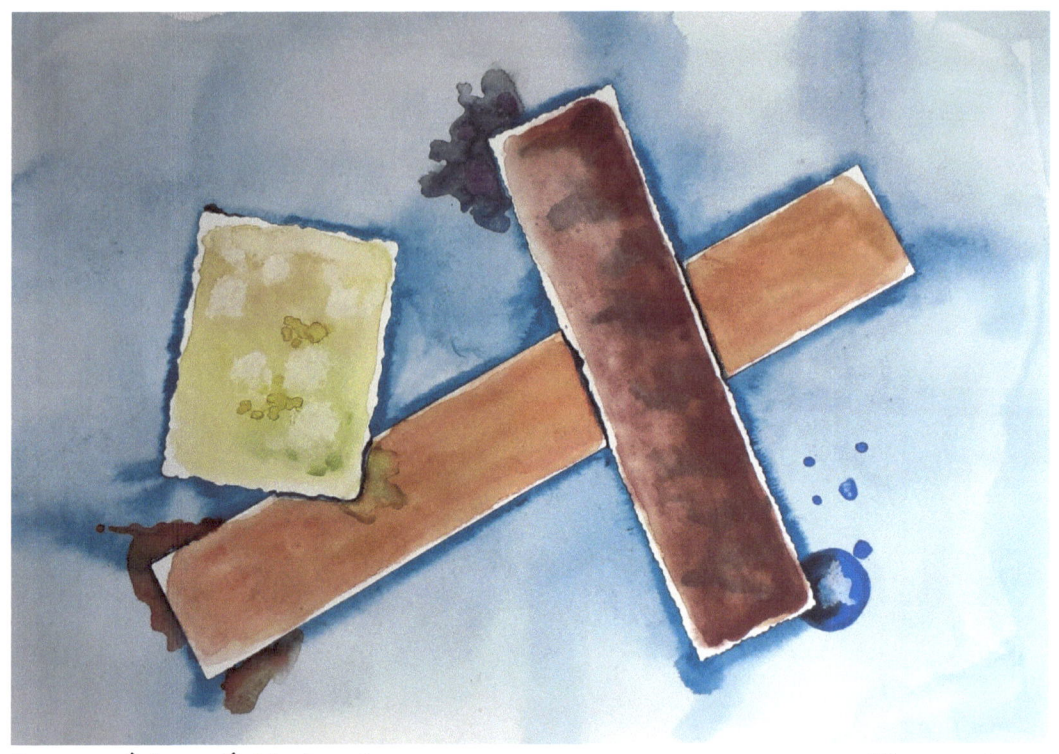

Cromer (almost) Abstract   **Watercolour**

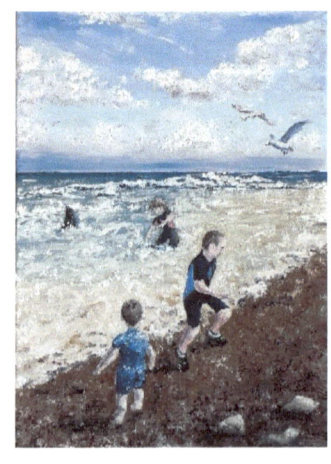

The idea of this task was to take a piece of work and use only the colours from it to create a painting with no relation or link to the original, or anything else in the physical world. I didn't quite meet the brief, but I like the result anyway.

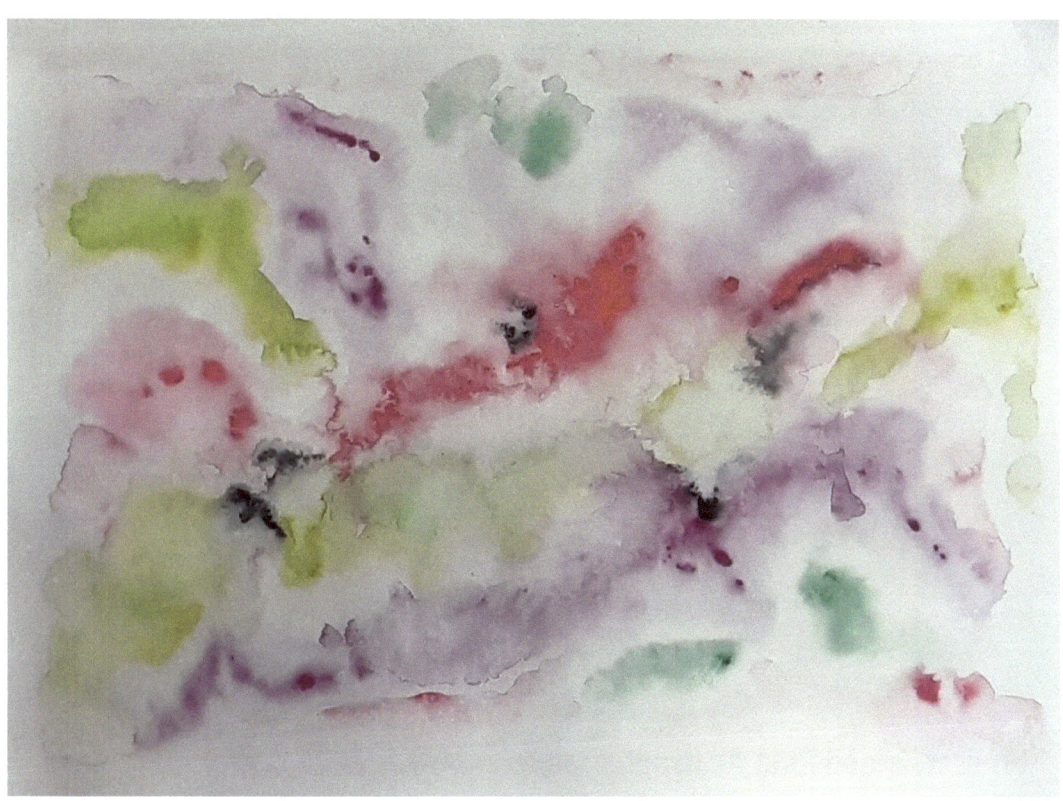

Tulips In Jug Abstract   **Watercolour**

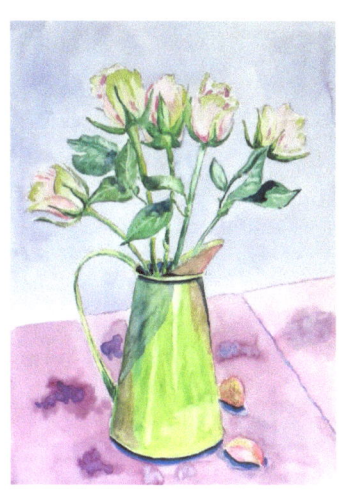

Continuing the Abstract colour theme

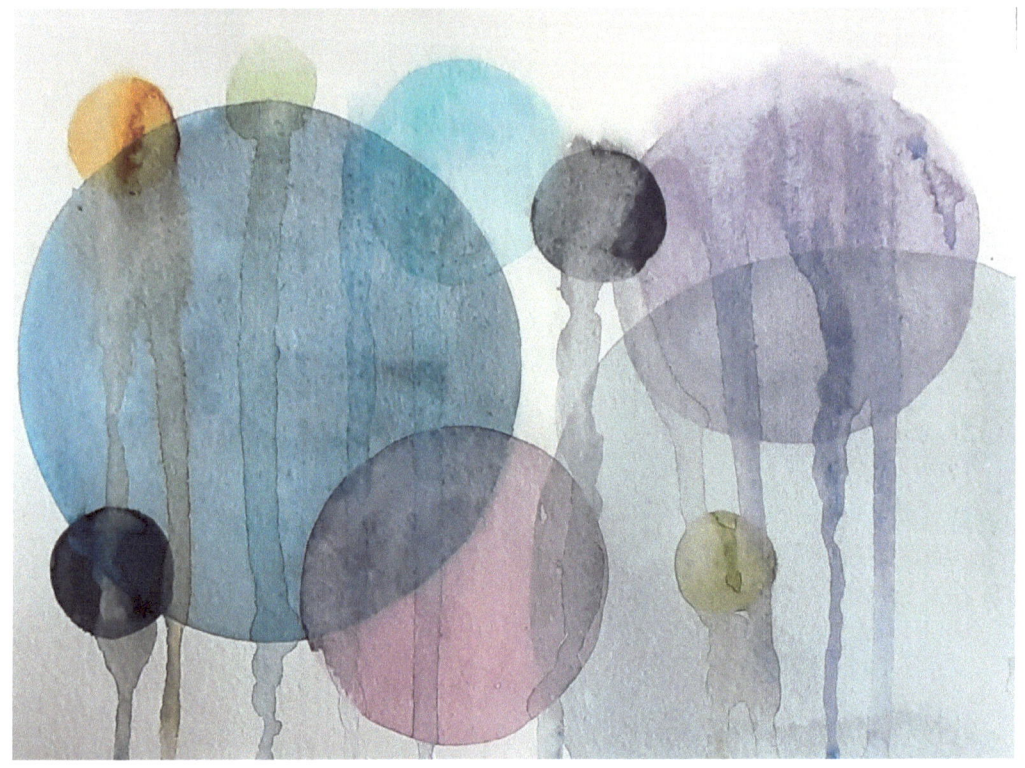

Umbrellas and Rain Abstract   Watercolour

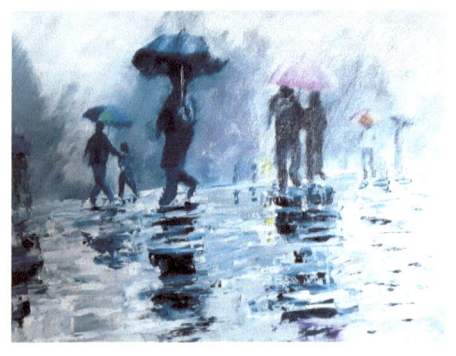

This abstract (using the colour from 'Rain' painting) was more difficult than it looks. I wanted the colour to run and mingle in a certain way but I had let it dry too much. I had to help the runs by adding more colour, all's well that ends well.

Thankyou

I really hope you have enjoyed a lighthearted look at my personal journey through learning to paint. I certainly haven't finished the ride yet, I still have a lot to learn and look forward to doing so. My hope is that this book will encourage others who have a hankering to learn and have been putting it off, to go ahead and begin. Join a class if you can, it makes all the difference and it's great to mix with others with the same interest. Good luck. and thankyou for reading.

About the Author

My name is Sandra and I live in Washington in the North East of England. I am originally from Coventry in the Midlands and moved North in the 1980's. I have a lovely, kind, caring husband, two wonderful daughters, four incredible 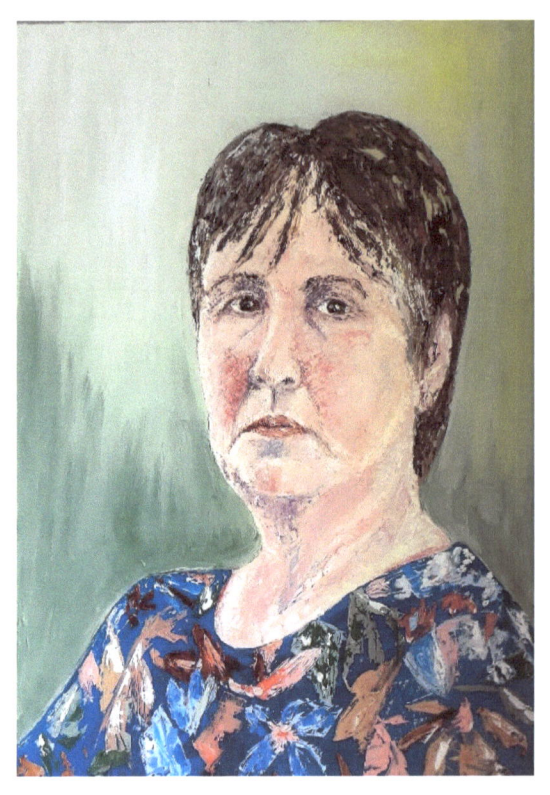 grandsons and one gorgeously perfect granddaughter, all of whom I am daily and forever grateful for. When I'm not spending time with those I love I am usually indulging in some sort of arts or crafts, and although I didn't take up painting until my mid fifties, I am certainly making up for lost time now. I can't get enough of it.

www.ingramcontent.com/pod-product-compliance
Lightning Source LLC
Chambersburg PA
CBHW051209220526
45473CB00003B/970